THE HOUND
OF THE BASKERVILLES

This is perhaps the most famous detective story in the world. Sherlock Holmes is certainly the most famous detective. Sir Arthur Conan Doyle created him almost a hundred years ago, but his adventures still seem fresh and exciting today.

To understand this story, you must understand Dartmoor, which is a real place in the south-west of England. It is a wild place of rocks and wet lands, where quite suddenly, on a beautiful sunny day, a thick mist can come down and hide everything. It is a place of green marsh – soft wet ground which can pull you down and drown you in deep black mud. It is where the British have their top security prison.

And it is the place where, many years ago, there was a huge and terrifying dog – the Hound of the Baskervilles.

OXFORD BOOKWORMS LIBRARY
Crime & Mystery

The Hound of the Baskervilles

Stage 4 (1400 headwords)

Series Editor: Jennifer Bassett
Founder Editor: Tricia Hedge
Activities Editors: Jennifer Bassett and Alison Baxter

SIR ARTHUR CONAN DOYLE

The Hound
of the Baskervilles

Retold by
Patrick Nobes

OXFORD UNIVERSITY PRESS
2000

Oxford University Press
Great Clarendon Street, Oxford OX2 6DP

Oxford New York
Athens Auckland Bangkok Bogotá Buenos Aires Calcutta Cape Town
Chennai Dar es Salaam Delhi Florence Hong Kong Istanbul Karachi
Kuala Lumpur Madrid Melbourne Mexico City Mumbai Nairobi
Paris São Paulo Shanghai Singapore Taipei Tokyo Toronto Warsaw
and associated companies in
Berlin Ibadan

OXFORD and OXFORD ENGLISH
are trade marks of Oxford University Press

ISBN 0 19 423035 X

This simplified edition © Oxford University Press 2000

Fourth impression 2000

First published in Oxford Bookworms 1989
This second edition published in the Oxford Bookworms Library 2000

A complete recording of this Bookworms edition of *The Hound of the
Baskervilles* is available on cassette ISBN 0 19 422699 9

The publishers would like to thank the Mary Evans Picture Library
for their permission to reproduce illustrations.

Printed in Spain by Unigraf s.l.

CONTENTS

1

The Case Begins

The September sun was shining brightly into the windows of 221B Baker Street, and London was enjoying a beautiful late summer. I had finished my breakfast and was reading the newspaper. As usual, Holmes had got up late, and was still eating. We were expecting a visitor at half-past ten, and I wondered whether Holmes would finish his breakfast before our visitor arrived.

Holmes was in no hurry. He was reading once again a letter he had received three days ago. It was from Dr James Mortimer, who asked for an appointment with Holmes.

'Well, Watson,' Holmes said to me, 'I'm afraid that a doctor from Devonshire won't bring us anything of real interest. His letter doesn't tell us anything about his business though he says it's very important. I hope we can help him.'

At exactly half-past ten there was a knock on our front door.

'Good,' said Holmes. 'Dr Mortimer is clearly a man who will not waste our time.'

We stood up as our visitor was brought into the room.

'Good morning, gentlemen,' he said. 'I'm Dr James Mortimer, from Grimpen in Devonshire, and I think you must be Mr Sherlock Holmes.' He shook hands with Holmes, who said:

'How do you do, Dr Mortimer? May I introduce my good friend, Dr John Watson, who helps me with my cases. I hope you will allow him to listen to our conversation.'

'Of course,' said Mortimer, as he turned to me and shook hands. 'I need your help very badly, Mr Holmes. If it will be useful for Dr Watson to hear what I have to say, please let him stay and listen.'

Mortimer did not look like a country doctor. He was very tall and thin. He had a long thin nose. His grey eyes were bright, and he wore gold glasses. His coat and trousers were old and worn. His face was young, but his shoulders were bent like an old man's and his head was pushed forward. He took some papers from his pocket, and said:

'Mr Holmes, I need your help and advice. Something very strange and frightening has been happening.'

'Sit down, Dr Mortimer,' said Holmes, 'and tell us your problem. I'll help you if I can.'

2

The Baskerville Papers

'These papers were given to me by Sir Charles Baskerville,' said Dr Mortimer. 'He asked me to take good care of them. You may remember that Sir Charles died suddenly three months ago. His death caused much excitement in

2

Devonshire, the county where Baskerville Hall is. Sir Charles was a sensible man, but he believed the story which is told in these papers.'

Dr Mortimer went on: 'The story is about the Baskerville family. I have come to see you because I need your help. I think that something terrible is going to happen in the next twenty-four hours. But you can't help me unless you know the story in these papers. May I read them to you?'

'Please continue, Dr Mortimer,' said Holmes, and sat back in his chair with his eyes shut.

Mortimer began to read in his high, rather strange, voice:

I, William Baskerville, write this for my sons in the year 1742. My father told me about the Hound of the Baskervilles. He told me when it was first seen, and I believe his story was true. I want you, my sons, to read this story carefully. I want you to know that God punishes those who do evil. But never forget that He will forgive those who are sorry for any evil they have done.

A hundred years ago, in 1640, the head of the Baskerville family was Sir Hugo Baskerville. He was a wild and evil man. He was cruel and enjoyed hurting people. Sir Hugo fell in love with the daughter of a farmer who was a neighbour of his. The young woman was afraid of the evil Hugo, and avoided him. One day, Hugo heard that her father and brothers were away. He knew that she would be alone. So he rode to the farm with five or six of his evil friends. They made the girl go back to Baskerville Hall with them, and locked her in a room upstairs. Then they sat down in the great dining hall to drink. As usual, they drank bottle after bottle and soon they began to sing and laugh and shout evil words.

The girl upstairs, who was already very frightened, felt desperate when she heard the terrible things they were shouting. So she did a very brave thing. She opened the window, climbed out of the room and down the ivy on the wall. Then she started to run across the moor towards her home.

A little while later, Hugo left his friends and went upstairs to the room to take her some food and drink. When he found an open window and an empty room, he behaved like a man who was mad. He ran down the stairs. He screamed that he would give himself to the Devil if he caught the girl before she reached home. Some of Hugo's drunken friends told him to let the hounds chase her, and so he ran from the house and unlocked the dogs. Then he jumped on to his black horse, and rode off over the moor with the hounds running and crying around him.

Hugo's friends fetched their horses and followed him. There were thirteen of them. After a mile or two they passed an old farmer and asked him if he had seen Sir Hugo and the hounds. The man looked half

4

mad with fear and spoke with difficulty. He said that he had seen the girl and the hounds running close behind her. Sir Hugo had been riding just behind the hounds. 'But I have seen more than that,' the old man said. 'Behind Sir Hugo I saw a huge and terrible hound running silently. May God keep me safe from that hound of hell.'

The thirteen men laughed at the old man and rode on. But their laughter soon stopped when they saw Sir Hugo's horse running wildly towards them without a rider.

The thirteen men moved closer together as they rode on. They were suddenly afraid. Over the moor they went until, at last, they caught up with the hounds.

Everyone in the county knew that the Baskerville hounds were brave and strong. But now they were standing at the head of a deep valley in the moor with their ears and tails down. They were very frightened. Hugo's friends stopped. Most of them would not go on, but three were brave enough to go down into the valley.

The valley had a wide flat floor. In the middle of the flat ground stood two great stones. They had stood there for thousands of years. The moon was shining brightly on the great stones, and between them, on the flat ground, lay the girl. She had fallen there, dead of fear and exhaustion. Sir Hugo's body was lying

'Behind Sir Hugo I saw a huge and terrible hound.'

near her. But it was not the sight of Sir Hugo or the girl that filled the men with fear. It was the sight of the huge animal that was standing over Sir Hugo. Its teeth were at his throat. It was a great black creature that looked like a hound. But it was larger than any hound they had ever seen.

As they watched, it tore out Hugo Baskerville's throat. Then it turned towards them. Its eyes were burning brightly. Its body shone with a strange light. Blood ran from its mouth. The men screamed and kicked their horses. They rode back up the valley as fast as they could go. Later that night one died from the horror he had seen. The other two were mad for the rest of their lives.

That was the first time the Hound appeared, my sons. It has been seen many times since then, and many of the Baskervilles have died in strange and terrible ways. Because of this I warn you not to cross the moors at night. The Devil finds it easy to do his work when the world is dark.

3

How Sir Charles Died

When Dr Mortimer had finished reading this strange story, he looked across at Sherlock Holmes. Holmes looked bored.

'Did you find the story interesting?' asked Dr Mortimer.

'It may interest a collector of stories to frighten children,' said Holmes.

Dr Mortimer took a newspaper from another pocket.

'Now, Mr Holmes, let me read you something which was written only three months ago. It is from the Devonshire County newspaper, and it is about the death of Sir Charles Baskerville.'

Holmes looked more interested. Dr Mortimer began to read:

The sudden death of Sir Charles Baskerville has caused great sadness in the county. Although he had lived at Baskerville Hall for only two years, everyone liked him. Sir Charles had lived abroad and made his money there. He came back to spend his fortune on repairing Baskerville Hall and its farms and villages, as the buildings and lands were in very poor condition. He was a friendly and generous man, who gave freely to the poor.

The official report of his death does not explain everything that happened. However, it does show that there was no question of murder. Sir Charles died from natural causes, and the strange stories people are telling about his death are not true. His friend and doctor, Dr James Mortimer, said that Sir Charles' heart had been weak for some time.

The facts are simple. Every night before going to

bed, Sir Charles went for a walk in the gardens of Baskerville Hall. His favourite walk was down a path between two hedges of yew trees, the famous Yew Alley of Baskerville Hall. On the night of 4th June he went out for his walk to think and to smoke his usual cigar.

Sir Charles was going to London on the next day, and Barrymore, his butler, was packing his suitcases. By midnight Barrymore was worried that Sir Charles had not returned, so he went to look for him. He found the door of the Hall open. The day had been rainy and wet so Barrymore saw the prints left by Sir Charles' shoes as he had walked down the Alley. Half-way down the Alley is a gate, which leads to the moor. There were signs that Sir Charles had stood there for some time. Barrymore followed the footprints to the far end of the Alley. And there he found Sir Charles' body.

Barrymore reported something interesting about the footprints. He said that they changed between the moor gate and the end of the Alley. As far as the moor gate there was a whole footprint for each of Sir Charles' steps. After he passed the gate, only toe prints could be seen. Barrymore thought that Sir Charles had walked on his toes.

A man called Murphy, who buys and sells horses, was not far away at the time of Sir Charles' death. He had been drinking a lot of beer, but he says he heard cries. He is not sure where they came from.

Dr Mortimer was called to look at Sir Charles' body. There were no signs that Sir Charles had been murdered, but Dr Mortimer did not recognize his friend's face. The whole shape of it was changed. However, this often happens with deaths which are caused by weak hearts. When Dr Mortimer looked at the body, he found that this was, in fact, what had happened. Sir Charles' weak heart had failed, and this had caused his death.

Everyone hopes that the new head of the Baskerville family will move quickly into the Hall. Sir Charles' good work must go on.

The new head of the Baskerville family will be Sir Henry Baskerville, if he is still alive and if the lawyers can find him. He is the son of Sir Charles Baskerville's younger brother, who died some years ago. The young man has been living in the USA. The Baskerville lawyers are trying to contact him to tell him about his good fortune.

Dr Mortimer put the newspaper back into his pocket.

'Those are the official facts about the death of Sir Charles. They are the facts that everyone knows, Mr Holmes,' he said.

'Thank you for informing me about this interesting case,' Holmes said. 'I read about it at the time, but I heard none of the details. The newspaper gives the facts that everybody knows. Now I want you to tell me all the other

10

facts that *you* know. What do you know about the strange stories?'

'I haven't told anyone these other facts,' said Dr Mortimer. 'I am a man of science, as you know. I have always believed that there are sensible explanations for everything. I didn't want to say anything that could stop Sir Henry from coming to live at the Hall. But I will tell you the details that were not in the report.

'In the months before his death,' Dr Mortimer went on, 'Sir Charles was a very worried man. He was near to breaking down. He believed the story of the Hound of the Baskervilles. He refused to go out at night. He often asked me whether I had seen any strange animal or heard the cry of a hound on the moor at night. He always got very excited when he asked this question.

'I remember driving up to the Hall one evening about three weeks before he died. He was standing at the door. I went up to him, and saw him staring at something behind me. There was a look of horror on his face. I turned quickly and saw something moving between the trees. It looked like a small black cow. He was so frightened that I went to look for the animal. It had disappeared but Sir Charles was very worried. I stayed with him all the evening. It was then he gave me the old papers I have read to you. What I saw that evening may be important when you consider what happened on the night of his death.

'When Barrymore, the butler, found Sir Charles' body,

'I saw Sir Charles staring at something behind me.'

he sent someone to fetch me. I checked all the facts. I have just read them to you, and they are all true.

'But Barrymore said one thing that was not true. He said that there were no other prints on the ground around the body. He did not notice any. But I did. They were not close to the body, but they were fresh and clear.'

'Footprints?' asked Holmes.

'Yes. Footprints,' said Mortimer.

'A man's or a woman's?' asked Holmes.

Dr Mortimer looked at us strangely for a moment. His voice became a whisper as he answered:

'Mr Holmes, they were the footprints of a huge hound!'

The Problem

I felt a moment of fear as Mortimer spoke these words. Holmes sat forward in his excitement, and his eyes showed he was very interested indeed.

'Why did nobody else see these footprints?' he asked.

'The footprints were about twenty metres from the body, and nobody thought of looking so far away,' Mortimer replied.

'Are there many sheep dogs on the moor?' asked Holmes.

'Yes, but this was no sheep dog. The footprints were very large indeed – enormous,' Mortimer answered.

'But it had not gone near the body?'

'No.'

'What kind of night was it?' Holmes asked.

'It was wet and cold, though it wasn't actually raining.'

'Describe the Alley to me.'

'The Alley is a path between two long yew hedges. The hedges are small trees that were planted very close together. They are about four metres high. The distance between the two yew hedges is about seven metres. Down the middle is a path of small stones. The path is about three metres wide, with grass on each side of it.'

'I understand there is a gate through the hedge in one place,' said Holmes.

'Yes, there is a small gate, which leads to the moor.'

'Is there any other opening through the hedge?'

'No.'

'So you can enter or leave the Yew Alley only from the Hall, or through the moor gate?' asked Holmes.

'There is a way out through a summer house at the far end.'

'Had Sir Charles reached the summer house?'

'No. He lay about fifty metres from it,' said Mortimer.

'Now, Dr Mortimer, this is important. You say that the footprints you saw were on the path and not on the grass?'

'No footprints could show on the grass,' said Mortimer.

'Were they on the same side of the path as the moor gate?'

'Yes. They were.'

'I find that very interesting indeed. Another question: was the moor gate closed?'

'Yes. It was closed and locked.'

'How high is it?' asked Holmes.

'It is just over a metre high.'

'Then anyone could climb over it?'

'Yes.'

'What prints did you see by the moor gate?'

'Sir Charles seems to have stood there for five or ten minutes,' said Mortimer. 'I know that because his cigar had burned down and the ash had dropped twice off the end of it.'

'Excellent,' said Holmes. 'This man is a very good detective, Watson.'

'Sir Charles had left his footprints all over that little bit of the path where he was standing. I couldn't see any other prints.'

Sherlock Holmes hit his knee with his hand angrily.

'I like to look closely at these things myself,' he said. 'Oh, Dr Mortimer, why didn't you call me immediately?'

'Mr Holmes, the best detective in the world can't help with some things,' said Mortimer.

'You mean things that are outside the laws of nature – supernatural things?' asked Holmes.

'I didn't say so exactly,' replied Mortimer. 'But since Sir Charles died, I have heard about a number of things that seem to be supernatural. Several people have seen an animal on the moor that looks like an enormous hound. They all agree that it was a huge creature, which shone with a strange light like a ghost. I have questioned these people carefully. They are all sensible people. They all tell the same story. Although they have only seen the creature far away, it is exactly like the hell-hound of the Baskerville story. The people are very frightened, and only the bravest man will cross the moor at night.'

'And you, a man of science, believe that the creature is supernatural – something from another world?' asked Holmes.

'I don't know what to believe,' said Dr Mortimer.

'But you must agree that the footprints were made by a living creature, not a ghost?'

'When the hound first appeared two hundred and fifty

years ago, it was real enough to tear out Sir Hugo's throat
. . . but it was a supernatural hell-hound,' said Dr Mortimer.

'If you think that Sir Charles' death was caused by
something supernatural, my detective work can't help
you,' said Holmes, rather coldly.

'Perhaps,' said Mortimer. 'But you can help me by
advising me what to do for Sir Henry Baskerville. He
arrives in London by train in exactly', Dr Mortimer looked
at his watch, 'one hour and a quarter.'

'Sir Henry is now head of the Baskerville family?' asked
Holmes.

'Yes,' said Dr Mortimer. 'He is the last of the Baskervilles.
The family lawyers contacted him in the USA. He has
come to England immediately by ship. He landed this
morning. Now, Mr Holmes, what do you advise me to do
with him?'

'Why should he not go to the family home?' asked
Holmes.

'Because so many Baskervilles who go there die horrible
deaths. But Sir Charles' good work must go on. If it
doesn't, all the people on the Baskerville lands will be
much poorer. If the Baskerville family leaves the Hall, that
is what will happen. I don't know what to do. That is why
I came to you for advice.'

Holmes thought for a little while. Then he said: 'You
think it is too dangerous for any Baskerville to live at the
Hall because of this supernatural hell-hound. Well, I think
you should go and meet Sir Henry Baskerville. Say nothing

to him about this. I shall give you my advice in twenty-four hours. At ten o'clock tomorrow morning, Dr Mortimer, I would like you to bring Sir Henry Baskerville here.'

Dr Mortimer got up from his chair. As he was leaving the room, Holmes said: 'One more question, Dr Mortimer. You said that before Sir Charles' death several people saw this strange creature on the moor?'

'Three people did,' said Mortimer.

'Did anyone see it after the death?'

'I haven't heard of anyone.'

'Thank you, Dr Mortimer. Good morning.'

After Mortimer had left us, Holmes sat down in his chair. He looked pleased. He always looked pleased when a case interested him.

I knew that he needed to be alone to think about all that he had heard. I went out for the day, and came back to find the room full of thick smoke from Holmes' pipe.

'What do you think of this case?' I asked him.

'It is hard to say. Take, for example, the change in the footprints. Did Sir Charles walk on his toes down the Alley? Only a stupid person is likely to believe that. The truth is he was running – running for his life. He ran until his heart stopped and he fell dead.'

'What was he running from?' I asked.

'That is the difficult question,' said Holmes. 'I think he was mad with fear before he began to run. He didn't know what he was doing. That explains why he ran away from the house instead of towards it. He was running away from help. The next question: who was he waiting for that night? And why was he waiting in the Yew Alley and not in the house?'

'You think he was waiting for someone?'

'Sir Charles was old and unwell. We can understand why he took a walk each evening. But why did he stand in the cold, on wet ground, for five or ten minutes? Dr Mortimer cleverly noted the cigar ash, so we know how long Sir Charles stood there. We know that he kept away from the moor, so it's unlikely that he waited at the moor gate every evening. I am beginning to understand some things, Watson. But I'll think no more about it until we meet Dr Mortimer and Sir Henry Baskerville in the morning. Please give me my violin.'

And Holmes began to play his violin. He had done all the thinking he could. Now he needed more details of the case to help him.

5

Sir Henry Baskerville

Dr Mortimer and Sir Henry Baskerville arrived at exactly ten o'clock the following morning. Sir Henry was a small, healthy, well-built man. His face showed that he had a strong character. He wore a country suit of thick, red-brown material, and his skin showed that he spent most of his time in the open air.

'I am glad this meeting was already arranged,' Sir Henry said, after we had shaken hands with our visitors. 'I need your help, Mr Holmes. A strange thing happened to me this morning. Look at this letter.'

He put a piece of paper on the table. On it were the words: 'Do not go on to the moor. If you do, your life will be in danger.' The words had been cut out of a newspaper.

'Can you tell me, Mr Holmes, what this means, and who is so interested in me?' Sir Henry asked.

'This is very interesting,' said Holmes. 'Look how badly it has been done. I think the writer was in a hurry. Why? Perhaps because he did not want somebody to see him. I think the address was written in a hotel. The pen and the ink have both given the writer trouble. The pen has run dry three times in writing a short address. There was probably very little ink in the bottle. A private pen and bottle of ink are never allowed to get into that condition. Hullo, what's this?'

He was holding the letter only a few centimetres from his eyes.

'Well?' I asked.

'Nothing,' he said, and threw the letter down. 'Now, Sir Henry, have you anything else to tell us?'

'No,' said Sir Henry. 'Except that I have lost one of my shoes. I put a pair outside my door last night. I wanted the hotel to clean them, but when I went to get them this morning, one had gone. I only bought them yesterday, and I have never worn them. But I wanted a good shine on them.'

'One shoe seems a useless thing to steal,' said Holmes. 'I am sure the shoe will be found in the hotel and returned to you. But now we must tell you some things about the Baskerville family.'

Dr Mortimer took out the old Baskerville papers and read them to Sir Henry. Holmes then told him about the death of Sir Charles.

'So this letter is from someone who is trying to warn me, or frighten me away,' said Sir Henry.

'Yes,' said Holmes. 'And we have to decide if it is sensible for you to go to Baskerville Hall. There seems to be danger there for you.'

'There is no man or devil who will stop me from going to the home of my family,' said Sir Henry angrily. 'I want some time to think about what you have told me. Will you and Dr Watson join me for lunch at my hotel in two hours' time? By then, I'll be able to tell you what I think.'

Dr Mortimer and Sir Henry said goodbye, and decided to walk back to their hotel.

As soon as our visitors had gone, Holmes changed from the talker to the man of action.

'Quick, Watson. Your coat and hat. We must follow them.' We got ready quickly and went into the street. Our friends were not far ahead of us and we followed. We stayed about a hundred metres behind them.

Suddenly Holmes gave a cry. I saw a taxi driving along very slowly on the other side of the road from our friends.

'That's our man, Watson! Come along!'

'That's our man, Watson! Come along! We'll have a good look at him.'

I saw a man with a large black beard looking out of the taxi window. He had been following and watching our friends. But when he saw us running towards him, he shouted something to the driver, and the taxi drove off quickly down the road. Holmes looked round for another taxi, but could not see one. He began to run after the first taxi, but it was soon out of sight.

'Well, I got the number of the taxi,' said Holmes. 'So I can find the driver. He may be able to tell us something about his passenger. Would you recognize the man if you saw him again?'

'Only his beard,' I said.

'He wanted us to recognize the beard,' said Holmes. 'I think it was a false one.'

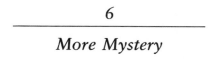

6

More Mystery

Later, we went on to Sir Henry's hotel. He was pleased to see us, but rather angry because another of his shoes had disappeared. This time it was one shoe of an old pair. I could see that Holmes found this both interesting and strange. He thought about it for a few moments, but said nothing except that he did not understand why a second shoe had been stolen.

At lunch, Sir Henry told Holmes that he had decided to go to Baskerville Hall.

'I think you have decided to do the right thing,' said Holmes. 'I know somebody is following you. If someone tries to harm you in London, it will be hard to stop him or catch him afterwards. In the country we have a better chance.'

Holmes went on to tell them about what we had seen that morning. Then he asked Dr Mortimer if anyone with a large black beard lived in or near Baskerville Hall.

'Yes,' said Dr Mortimer, 'Barrymore, Sir Charles' butler, has a black beard.'

'We must check whether Barrymore is in London or at Baskerville Hall,' said Holmes. 'I shall send a telegram to Barrymore at the Hall, which will say: "Is everything ready for Sir Henry?" Then I'll send another telegram to the local post office. This one will say: "Please put telegram to Mr Barrymore into his own hand. If he is away, please return telegram to Sir Henry Baskerville." I'll give your address at this hotel. We shall know before evening whether Barrymore is in Devonshire or not.'

'Barrymore and his wife have a very fine home and nothing to do while the family is not living in the Hall,' said Sir Henry.

'That's true,' said Holmes. 'Did the Barrymores receive anything from Sir Charles' will? And did they know that they would get some money when he died?'

'Yes,' said Dr Mortimer. 'They each received £500, and

Sir Charles told everyone what he had written in his will.'

'That's very interesting,' said Holmes.

'I hope you don't suspect everyone who got something from the will,' said Dr Mortimer. 'I received £1,000.'

'Indeed!' said Holmes. 'And who else received money?'

'A lot of people received a little money. He gave a lot of money to a number of hospitals. The rest all went to Sir Henry, who received £740,000.'

'I had no idea it was so much,' said Holmes in surprise.

'The Baskerville lands are worth about one million pounds,' Dr Mortimer said.

'Dear me,' said Holmes. 'A man could kill for that much. One more question. If something happened to our young friend here, who would get Baskerville Hall and all its lands?'

'Well, as you know, Sir Charles had two brothers. Sir Henry is the only son of Sir Charles' younger brother. The youngest brother of the three, Roger, was a criminal. The police wanted him, so he had to leave England. They say he looked exactly like the family picture of old Sir Hugo, who first saw the Hound. He was the same kind of man, too. He went to South America, where he died of a fever. So if Sir Henry died, Baskerville Hall would go to James Desmond, who is a cousin of the Baskervilles. James Desmond is an old man, who lives in the north of England. His life is very simple and he would not want to be rich.'

'Thank you, Dr Mortimer,' said Holmes. 'Now, Sir Henry, I agree that you should go to Baskerville Hall as quickly as possible. But you must not go alone. I myself cannot leave London at the present time. I am working on another case. I am trying to save one of the most important men in England from a difficult situation. I hope my friend Watson will go with you. If there is danger, you could not have a better man by your side.'

Sir Henry and I were both very happy with this idea. So we arranged to travel to Devonshire on the following Saturday.

Just as we were leaving Sir Henry's room, he gave a cry and got down on his knees by the table.

'Here's my brown shoe that was lost,' he said, reaching under the table.

'That's very strange,' said Dr Mortimer. 'We both searched the room before lunch, and it wasn't under the table then.'

None of the people who worked at the hotel could explain how the shoe had got back into the room.

So we had another mystery. On the way back to Baker Street in the taxi, Holmes sat thinking deeply. All through the afternoon and the evening he went on thinking silently, and smoking pipe after pipe.

Just before dinner, a telegram arrived. It was from Sir Henry and said: 'Have just heard that Barrymore is at the Hall.'

'So we don't have the answer to the mystery of the man with the beard,' said Holmes. 'But perhaps we shall soon have an answer to another question.'

25

At that moment the door bell rang. It was the driver of the bearded man's taxi.

'I got a message that you wanted to see me,' said the driver. 'I hope there's nothing wrong.'

'No, no, my good man,' said Holmes. 'In fact I'll give you some money if you can answer my questions clearly. Tell me all about the man in your taxi this morning. He was watching this house at ten o'clock and then told you to follow the two gentlemen who came out of it.'

The taxi driver was surprised at how much Holmes seemed to know. He answered: 'The man told me that he was a detective, and that I should say nothing about him to anyone.'

'This is a serious business,' said Holmes, 'and you will be in trouble if you try to hide anything. What can you tell me?'

'The man told me his name,' said the driver.

Holmes looked like a man who has just won an important game. 'That was not very clever of him,' he said. 'What was his name?'

'His name,' said the taxi driver, 'was Sherlock Holmes.'

I have never seen my friend look more surprised. Then he laughed loudly. 'Tell me where he got into your taxi and everything that happened.'

We already knew most of what the taxi driver told us. But we learned that after we had lost sight of the taxi, it had gone to Waterloo station, where the man had caught his train. The taxi driver said that the man was well-dressed and had a black beard and pale face. He was about forty and not very tall. The driver did not know the colour of the man's eyes.

Holmes gave the man a pound, and sent him away. Then he said:

'We have a very clever enemy, Watson. He is winning the game at the moment. We have no answers at all to the strange things that have happened in London. I hope you are more successful at Baskerville Hall, but I am not happy about sending you there. There is too much danger in this case.'

7

Baskerville Hall

Holmes came to Waterloo station to say goodbye to us. Our friends told him that they were sure nobody had followed them since our last meeting. Sir Henry's other shoe had not reappeared. Holmes repeated his warning that Sir Henry should not go on the moor at night, and should not go anywhere alone. Then Holmes checked with me that I had my gun, an army revolver.

The journey was fast and enjoyable. We were met at Newtown station and driven to Baskerville Hall. The countryside we drove through was beautiful, but behind it we could see the long, dark, frightening hills of the moor.

We were now on the cold, open moor.

As we turned a corner, we were surprised to see a soldier on horseback. He was carrying a gun.

Dr Mortimer asked our driver why the soldier was there.

'A dangerous criminal has escaped from the prison, sir,' he told us. 'He's been free for three days now, and people are frightened. His name is Selden. He's the man who did that murder in London.'

I remembered the case well. It had been a very cruel murder. I thought of this killer out on the empty, wild moor, and I felt more and more uncomfortable about my surroundings. The beautiful green fields with their thick hedges were behind us, and we were now on the cold, open moor. Everything was grey, hard and wild. Huge rough stones stood on the hard ground. The tops of the hills stood sharply like cruel teeth against the sky. A cold wind was blowing, and night was falling. I saw Sir Henry pull his coat closer round him.

At last we reached the gates of Baskerville Hall. From the gates a long, dark road led up to the house, with the black shapes of old trees on each side of it. At the end of this road we could see the great house standing with a pale light round it like a ghost.

'I can understand why my uncle felt that trouble was coming to him here. It's not a welcoming place,' said Sir Henry, and his voice shook as he spoke.

As we got closer, we could see that the Hall was a heavy, dark building with a large main entrance. Most of the building was old and was covered in dark green ivy, but some of it had been built more recently and was of grim, black stone. A dull light shone through the heavy windows. Black smoke was coming from one of the high chimneys of the main building.

'Welcome, Sir Henry! Welcome to Baskerville Hall.'

Barrymore, the butler, and his wife were waiting on the steps at the main entrance. They came down and took our suitcases into the house. Dr Mortimer left us to go home, and we went into the hall, where a fire was burning. It was a fine room, large and high.

'It's exactly as I imagined an old family home,' Sir Henry said.

Barrymore showed us to our rooms. He was a tall, handsome man, with a full black beard. After we had washed and changed our clothes, he brought our dinner. The dining room was not very welcoming. It needed more lights to make it brighter. On the walls were the pictures of the Baskervilles of the past. They looked down on us silently, and did nothing to make us feel happier.

After dinner we went to our rooms. Before I got into bed, I looked out of my window. A strong wind sang sadly as it bent the trees in front of the Hall. A half moon shone through the dark, flying clouds on to the wild and empty moor.

I could not sleep. Then, suddenly, in the middle of the night I heard very clearly the sound of a woman crying. It was the crying of a person who was hurt by some deep sadness. The sound was not far away, and was certainly in the house.

8

The Stapletons of Pen House

The next morning was sunny, and we were much more cheerful.

I told Sir Henry about the crying I had heard. He rang the bell to call Barrymore, and asked him if he could explain the crying. Barrymore's face went white when he heard Sir Henry's question.

'There are only two women in the house, Sir Henry,' he answered. 'One is the maid, who sleeps on the other side of the house. The other is my wife, and she was certainly not crying.'

But he was telling a lie. I saw Mrs Barrymore after breakfast. The sun was full on her face, and it was clear she had been crying.

Why had Barrymore lied? What deep sadness had made his wife cry? There was a mystery surrounding this black-bearded, handsome man. Was it possible that Barrymore was in fact the man who had been watching Sir Henry in London? I decided I must check with the local post office that the telegram had really been put into Barrymore's own hands.

While Sir Henry worked at some papers, I walked to the post office. It was in the nearest village, which was called Grimpen. I spoke to the boy who had taken the telegram to the Hall.

31

'Did you give it to Mr Barrymore himself?' I asked.

'Well,' the boy said, 'he was working up on the roof, so I couldn't give it to him. I gave it to Mrs Barrymore, and she promised to give it to him at once.'

'Did you see Mr Barrymore?' I asked him.

'No,' said the boy, 'but why did his wife say he was up on the roof if he wasn't?'

It was hopeless to ask any more questions. It was clear that Holmes' cleverness with the telegram had not given us the proof we needed.

I was walking away from the post office when I heard someone running after me. A voice called me by name, and I turned. I expected to see Dr Mortimer, as I knew nobody else in the village. To my surprise it was a stranger. He was a small, thin man, between thirty and forty years old, with fair hair and no beard. He was carrying a butterfly net, and a box for putting butterflies in.

'I hope you will excuse me for introducing myself, Dr Watson,' he said as he came up to me. 'My name is Stapleton. I was in Dr Mortimer's house and we saw you. He told me who you are. May I walk along with you? This path back to the Hall goes near my home, Pen House. Please come in and meet my sister, and spend an hour with us.'

I accepted Stapleton's invitation, and we walked together.

'I know that you are a close friend of Sherlock Holmes,' said Stapleton. 'Has Mr Holmes any ideas about Sir Charles' death?'

'I'm afraid I can't answer that question,' I said.

'Will Mr Holmes visit us himself?' he asked.

'He can't leave London at the moment,' I answered. I was rather surprised that he was asking me these questions.

We walked on. Stapleton told me that he and his sister had lived in Devonshire for only two years. They had moved there soon after Sir Charles had begun to live in Baskerville Hall. He also talked about the moor and how it

'That is the Great Grimpen Marsh.'

33

interested him. He told me to look across the moor to a place which was a bright green colour.

'That is the Great Grimpen Marsh,' he said. 'If animals or men go into the marsh, they will sink into it and die. But I can find my way to the very centre of it. Look, there is another of those poor horses.'

Something brown was fighting to get out of the bright green of the marsh. Then a terrible cry came across the moor. The horse's head and neck disappeared under the green.

'It's gone,' Stapleton said. 'The marsh has caught and killed it. That often happens. It is an evil place, the Great Grimpen Marsh.'

'But you say you can go safely in and out of it?' I asked him.

'Yes, there are a few paths, and I have found them. The low hills you can see are like islands surrounded by the marsh. That is where I can find the unusual plants and butterflies. And that's why I found my way through the marsh.'

'I shall try my luck one day,' I said.

He looked at me in surprise. 'Please don't try,' he said. 'You would never return alive, and it would be my fault.'

'Listen,' I said. 'What is that?'

A long, low cry, very deep and very sad, came over the moor. It filled the whole air. Then it died away.

'What is it?' I asked, with a cold fear in my heart.

Stapleton had a strange look on his face. 'The people say

it's the Hound of the Baskervilles, which is calling for something to hunt and kill. I've heard it once or twice before, but never so loud.'

'You are a man of science,' I said. 'You don't believe that, do you? Isn't there a natural explanation for the sound?'

'A marsh makes strange noises sometimes. It is the water and the wet ground moving.'

'But that was the voice of a living creature,' I said.

'Well, perhaps it was. There are some very unusual birds on the moors. It was most probably the cry of one of those.'

At that moment a small butterfly flew across the path in front of us. 'Excuse me, Dr Watson,' shouted Stapleton, and ran off to try to catch the butterfly. He ran quickly and followed the butterfly on to the marsh, but he knew exactly where he could go, and was not in any danger.

As I watched him, I heard the sound of steps behind me. I turned and saw a woman near me on the path. I was sure she was Miss Stapleton. She was very beautiful. She was dark and tall, with a lovely face. Before I could say anything, she said:

'Go back! Go straight back to London, immediately. I cannot tell you why, but please do what I ask you, and never come near the moor again. But my brother is coming. Not a word to him.'

Stapleton had caught the butterfly, and was walking back to us.

35

'Hello, my dear,' he said to his sister, but it seemed to me that his voice was not completely friendly. 'I see that you two have already introduced yourselves.'

'Yes,' she said. 'I was telling Sir Henry that it was rather late in the year for him to see the true beauty of the moor.'

'I am sorry,' I said. 'You have made a mistake. I'm not Sir Henry. I am a friend who is visiting him, and my name is Dr Watson.'

Miss Stapleton was clearly angry with herself. 'I'm sorry,' she said. 'Please forget what I said. But do come with us to our house.'

The house was lonely and rather grim. I wondered why the two of them had come to live so far away from anyone else. Stapleton seemed to know what I was thinking, and said: 'You may think this a lonely, strange place to live, but the moors are very interesting, and we enjoy it here. I owned a school in the north of England, but I had to close it. I miss the boys and girls, but there is plenty to do here, and we have good neighbours. I hope Sir Henry will become one of them. May I visit the Hall this afternoon to meet him, do you think?'

'I'm sure he will be very pleased to meet you,' I said. 'I must go back to the Hall now, and I shall tell him immediately.'

I said goodbye to the Stapletons, and continued on the path back to the Hall. I had been walking for only a few minutes when I was surprised to see Miss Stapleton sitting on a rock ahead of me. She was breathing quickly, and I realized she had run by a quicker way to get ahead of me.

'Dr Watson,' she said. 'I want to say sorry for the mistake I made. I thought you were Sir Henry. Please forget what I said. I did not mean you were in danger. Now I must go, or my brother will miss me.'

'I cannot forget your words, Miss Stapleton,' I said. 'If Sir Henry is in danger, I must tell him.'

'You know the story of the Hound?' she asked me.

'Yes, but I do not believe it,' I replied.

'But I think it's true,' she said. 'Please persuade Sir Henry to leave this place. So many of his family have died here mysteriously. He must not put his life in danger by staying here.'

'Sir Henry won't leave this place without a real reason,' I said.

'I can't give you a real reason. I don't know anything for certain.'

'One more question, Miss Stapleton,' I said. 'The story of the Hound is well known. Why didn't you want your brother to hear what you said?'

'My brother wants the head of the Baskerville family to live in the Hall,' she said. 'He wants Sir Henry to continue the good work that Sir Charles began. He doesn't want Sir Henry to go and live in another place. So he doesn't want me to talk about the Hound. I must go now, or my brother will guess I have been speaking to you. Good-bye!'

She turned and went back towards her house, and I walked on to Baskerville Hall.

9

The Escaped Prisoner

Mr Stapleton came to the Hall and met Sir Henry that same afternoon. The next morning he took us to the place where the evil Sir Hugo died. Then we had lunch at Pen House. Sir Henry clearly thought Miss Stapleton was very beautiful. His eyes followed her everywhere. He liked her very much, and I was sure that she felt the same about him. He spoke about her again and again as we walked home. After the first meeting, we met the Stapletons almost every day.

After a short time it was clear that Sir Henry had fallen deeply in love with the beautiful Miss Stapleton. At first I thought that Stapleton would be very pleased if his sister married Sir Henry. However, I soon realized that he did not want their friendship to grow into love. He did everything he could to make sure that they were never alone. On one or two occasions they did manage to meet alone, but Stapleton followed them and was not pleased to see them together.

I soon met another neighbour of Sir Henry's. His name was Mr Frankland, and he lived about four miles to the south of the Hall. He was an old man with a red face and white hair. He had two hobbies. The first was arguing. He argued with everybody. The second hobby was studying the stars. For this he had a very big telescope. For several days he had been watching the moor through the telescope. He wanted to find Selden, the escaped murderer. Nobody had seen the prisoner for a fortnight, and we all thought that he had probably left the moor.

A few nights later I was woken by a noise at about two in the morning. I heard someone walking softly outside my door. I got up, opened the door and looked out. I saw Barrymore moving carefully and quietly away from me. I followed him, as quietly as I could. He went into one of the empty bedrooms and left the door open. I went quietly up to the door and looked inside.

Barrymore was standing at the window. He was holding a light in his hand and looking out on to the moor. He stood without moving for a few minutes and then he put out the light.

I went quickly back to my room. A few minutes later I heard Barrymore go softly by.

The next morning I told Sir Henry what I had seen.

'We must follow him and find out what he is doing,' said Sir Henry. 'He won't hear us if we move carefully.'

That night we sat in Sir Henry's room and waited. At about three o'clock in the morning we heard the sound of footsteps outside the bedroom. We looked out and saw Barrymore. We followed him as quietly as we could. He went into the same room as before. We reached the door and looked in. There was Barrymore, with the light in his hand, looking out across the moor, exactly as I had seen him on the night before.

There was Barrymore, with the light in his hand.

Sir Henry walked into the room and said: 'What are you doing here, Barrymore?'

Barrymore turned round quickly, surprise and horror on his face.

'Nothing, sir,' he said. The shadows on the wall from his light were jumping up and down as his hand shook. 'It was the window, sir. I go round at night to see that they are closed, and this one wasn't shut.'

'Come now, Barrymore,' said Sir Henry. 'No lies. What were you doing with that light? You were holding it up to the window.'

I suddenly had an idea. 'I think he was sending a

message,' I said. 'Let's see if there's an answer from someone on the moor.'

I held the light up to the window, and looked out into the darkness. Suddenly a light answered from the moor.

'There it is,' I cried. I waved my light backwards and forwards across the window. The light on the moor answered by moving in the same way.

'Now, Barrymore, who is your friend on the moor? What's going on?'

'That's my business,' said Barrymore. 'I won't tell you.'

'Are you making some criminal plan against me?' Sir Henry said.

'No, it's nothing against you, sir,' said a voice from behind us. It was Mrs Barrymore. She had followed us and was standing at the door. 'He's doing it for me. My unhappy brother is cold and hungry on the moor. We cannot let him die. Our light is to tell him that food is ready for him. His light shows us where to take it.'

'Then your brother is . . .' began Sir Henry.

'The escaped prisoner, sir. Selden, the murderer. He is my younger brother. He has done evil things, but to me he is still the little boy I loved and cared for. I had to help him. Everything my husband has done has been for me. Please don't take his job from him. It's not his fault.'

Sir Henry turned to Barrymore and said:

'I cannot blame you for helping your wife. Go to bed, and we'll talk about this in the morning.'

The Barrymores left us.

'The murderer is waiting out there by that light,' said Sir Henry. 'He's a danger to everyone. I'm going to catch him. If you want to come with me, Watson, fetch your revolver and let's go.'

We left the Hall immediately.

'We must surprise him and catch him,' said Sir Henry. 'He's a dangerous man. Now, Watson, what would Holmes say about this? Do you remember what the old papers said? They said the Devil does his work when the world is dark.'

Just as he spoke there came a strange cry from across the moor. It was the same cry I had heard when I was with Stapleton on the edge of the Great Grimpen Marsh.

'What is that noise?' asked Sir Henry. He stopped and put his hand on my arm to hold me back.

'I've heard it before,' I said. 'Stapleton says it's the cry of a bird.'

'Watson,' said Sir Henry, his voice shaking, 'it is the cry of a hound. What do the local people say it is?'

'They say it is the cry of the Hound of the Baskervilles,' I replied.

'Can there possibly be some truth in the story?' said Sir Henry. 'Am I really in danger from such an evil thing? I think I am as brave as most men, but that sound froze my blood. But we have come out to catch that prisoner, and the Devil himself will not make me turn back.'

It was difficult to cross the moor in the dark, but at last we reached the light. It was standing on a rock. Suddenly an evil face, more like an animal than a man, looked at us from behind the rock. The escaped prisoner saw us and screamed as he turned to run.

Sir Henry and I were both good runners and very healthy men, but we soon realized that we had no chance of catching Selden. He knew the way, and was running for his life. Soon we had lost him in the dark, so we stopped and sat down, breathing heavily, to rest.

At that moment a very strange thing happened. The moon was low upon our right, and in its light we could see the top of a hill. On that hill, with the moon behind him, stood a tall, thin man. He was standing perfectly still. He was watching us.

It was not Selden, who had been running away from that hill. This man was much taller. With a cry of surprise I turned to Sir Henry. As I turned, the man disappeared.

I wanted to go across to the hill and search for him, but we were tired and I remembered that Sir Henry might be in danger. So we went back to Baskerville Hall.

Who was the tall man I had seen standing against the moon? Was he an enemy, or a friend who was watching over us?

I wished more and more that Holmes could leave London and come to Baskerville Hall. I wrote to him every few days and gave him the details of everything that happened and everyone I met.

10

The Letter

The following day was dull and foggy. The Hall was surrounded by heavy, low clouds, which opened now and then to show the grim, cold moor and its wet, grey rocks. The weather made us miserable. It was difficult to be cheerful when we felt danger all around us. I thought of Sir Charles' death, and the awful sound of the hound, which I had now heard twice. Holmes did not believe that there was a supernatural hound. But facts are facts, and I had heard a hound. Was there a huge hound living on the moor? If so, where could it hide? Where did it get its food? Why was it never seen by day? It was almost as difficult to accept a natural explanation as a supernatural explanation.

That morning Sir Henry and Barrymore argued about Selden, the escaped prisoner. Barrymore said that it was wrong to try to catch Selden.

'But the man is dangerous,' said Sir Henry. 'He'll do anything. Nobody is safe until he is in prison again. We must tell the police.'

'I promise he won't break into any house,' said Barrymore, 'and he won't cause any trouble. In a few days he will catch a boat for South America. Please don't tell the police about him. If you tell the police, my wife and I will be in serious trouble.'

'What do you say, Watson?' asked Sir Henry, turning to me.

'I don't think he will break into houses, or cause trouble. If he did, the police would know where to look for him and would catch him. He's not a stupid man.'

'I hope you're right,' said Sir Henry. 'I'm sure we're breaking the law. But I don't want to get Barrymore and his wife into trouble, so I shall not tell the police. I shall leave Selden in peace.'

Barrymore could not find the words to thank Sir Henry enough. Then he said: 'You have been so kind to us that I want to do something for you in return. I have never told anyone else. I know something more about poor Sir Charles' death.'

Sir Henry and I jumped up at once.

'Do you know how he died?' Sir Henry asked.

'No, sir, I don't know that, but I know why he was waiting at the gate. He was going to meet a woman.'

'Sir Charles was meeting a woman? Who was the woman?'

'I don't know her name,' Barrymore said, 'but it begins with L.L.'

'How do you know this, Barrymore?' I asked.

'Well, Sir Charles got a letter on the morning of the day he died. It was from Newtown, and the address was in a woman's writing. I forgot all about it, but some time after Sir Charles died my wife was cleaning the fireplace in his study. She found a letter. Most of it was burned, but the bottom of one page was not burned. On it was written: "Please, please, burn this letter, and be at the gate by ten o'clock. L.L." The paper fell into pieces as my wife went to move it. We don't know who L.L. is, but if you could find out, you might learn more about Sir Charles' death. We haven't told anyone else. We felt it would not be good for poor, kind Sir Charles. But we thought we ought to tell you, Sir Henry.'

The Barrymores left us and Sir Henry turned to me. 'If we can find L.L., the mystery may be at an end,' he said. 'What do you think we should do, Watson?'

'I must write to Holmes at once,' I said, and I went straight to my room and wrote a letter to Holmes, which gave him all the details of Barrymore's story.

On the following day heavy rain fell without stopping. I put on my coat and went for a long walk on the moor. I thought of Selden out on the cold moor in this weather. And I thought of the other man, the mysterious watcher.

As I walked, Dr Mortimer drove past me. He stopped and said he would take me back to the Hall.

'I expect you know almost everybody living near here,' I said. 'Do you know a woman whose names begin with the letters L.L.?'

Dr Mortimer thought for a minute, and then he said: 'Yes, Mrs Laura Lyons. She lives in Newtown.'

'Who is she?' I asked.

'She's Mr Frankland's daughter.'

'What, old Frankland who has the large telescope?'

'Yes,' said Dr Mortimer, 'Laura married a painter called Lyons who came to paint pictures of the moor. But he was cruel to her, and after a while he left her. Her father will not speak to her, because she married against his wishes. So her husband and her father have made her life very unhappy.'

'How does she live?' I asked.

'Several people who knew her sad story have helped her. Stapleton and Sir Charles gave her some money. I gave a little myself. She used the money to start a typewriting business.'

Dr Mortimer wanted to know why I was asking about Mrs Lyons. However, I preferred to keep the reason secret, and we talked about other things for the rest of the journey.

Only one other thing of interest happened that day. In the evening after dinner I had a few words with Barrymore alone. I asked him whether Selden had left the country.

'I don't know, sir,' Barrymore replied. 'I hope he has gone. But I've not heard anything of him since I last left food and some clothes for him, and that was three days ago.'

'Did you see him then?'

'No, sir, but the food and clothes were gone when I next went that way,' Barrymore told me.

'Then Selden was certainly there?' I asked.

'I think so, sir, unless the other man took everything.'

I sat very still and looked hard at Barrymore. 'You know there is another man, then? Have you seen him?'

'No, sir, but Selden told me about him a week or more ago. He is hiding from someone, too, but he is not an escaped prisoner. I don't like it, sir. Something evil is going to happen, I'm sure. Sir Henry would be much safer in London.'

'Did Selden tell you anything more about the other man?' I asked.

'He looked like a gentleman. He was living in one of the old stone huts on the moor. A boy works for him and brings him all the food and things he needs. That's all Selden told me.'

I thanked him, and he left me. I went to the window and looked out at the rain and the clouds. It was a wild night. I knew the huts Barrymore had spoken about. There were many of them on the moor. They had been built many hundreds of years ago by the people who lived on the moor. They would not keep a man warm and dry in bad weather. Selden could not choose to live anywhere else, but why did the other man live in such conditions?

I sat and thought what I should do next. I decided I must try to find the man who had been watching us. Was he the enemy who had been following us since the very beginning in London? If he was, and I could catch him, perhaps our difficulties would be at an end.

I also decided to hunt the man on my own. Sir Henry was still shaken by the terrible cry we had heard on the moor. I did not want to add to his troubles or to lead him into more danger.

11

Laura Lyons

I told Sir Henry about Laura Lyons, and that I wanted to speak to her as soon as possible. Then I went to her house in Newtown.

A maid took me into the sitting room, where a very

'What right have you to ask me about my private life?'

pretty lady with dark hair was working at a typewriter. I told her who I was, and that I had met her father.

'I have no contact with my father,' she said. 'He gave me no help when I was in trouble. Sir Charles Baskerville and some other kind people helped me when I was poor and hungry.'

'It is about Sir Charles that I have come to see you,' I said. 'I want to know if you ever wrote to him and asked him to meet you.'

She looked very angry, and her face went white.

'What a question!' she said. 'What right have you to ask me about my private life? But the answer is "no".'

'Surely you are not remembering clearly,' I said. 'I think you wrote to him on the day that he died. And your letter said: "Please, please, burn this letter, and be at the gate by ten o'clock".'

For a moment I thought she was going to faint. Then she said in a low voice: 'I asked Sir Charles to tell nobody.'

'You must not think that Sir Charles spoke to anyone about you,' I said. 'He put the letter on the fire, but not all of it was burnt. Now, did you write that letter to him?'

'Yes,' she said. 'Why should I be ashamed of writing to him? I wanted him to help me. I learned that he was going to London early on the following day, so I asked him to meet me before he went. I could not go to the Hall earlier that day.'

'But why did you ask him to meet you in the garden instead of in the house?' I asked.

'Do you think it would be sensible for a woman to go at that time of night into the house of an unmarried man?' she asked.

'Well, what happened when you got there?' I asked.

'I didn't go,' she replied.

'Mrs Lyons!'

'I tell you I did not go. Something happened that stopped me from going. I can't tell you what it was.'

'Mrs Lyons,' I said. 'If you did not see Sir Charles, you must tell me why. If you do not, it will look very bad for you if I have to go to the police with this new piece of information about the letter.'

Mrs Lyons thought for a moment, and then she said: 'I see that I must tell you. Perhaps you know that I married a man who was very cruel to me. I hate him and I wanted to get a divorce. But a divorce is expensive, and I had no money. I thought that if Sir Charles heard my sad story, he would help me to get a divorce.'

'Then why didn't you go to see Sir Charles?' I asked her.

'Because I got help from someone else,' she said.

'Why didn't you write to Sir Charles and tell him?'

'I was going to, but I saw in the newspaper the next morning that he had died.'

I asked Mrs Lyons a number of other questions, but she did not change her story, whatever I asked her. I was sure that she was telling the truth. I could check two important parts of the story. If they were right, there could be no doubt that she was telling the truth. I could check that she had begun to get her divorce at about the time of Sir Charles' death. I could also check that she had not been to Baskerville Hall on the night of Sir Charles' death.

But I was not sure that she had told me the whole truth. Why had she nearly fainted when I had told her about the letter? That was not completely explained by the story she had told me.

I had discovered all I could for the moment. I left her, and went to search for more information in a different place.

12

The Man on the Moor

I drove out of Newtown and went to begin my search for the mysterious man on the moor. There were hundreds of the old stone huts on the moor. Barrymore did not know in which of them the mysterious man was living. I had seen the man on the night when Sir Henry and I had chased Selden, so I decided to start my search near that place.

The path I took ran past Mr Frankland's house, and I saw him standing at his gate. He called to me, and invited me to go in and have a drink with him. He had been arguing with the police, and was angry with them. He began to tell me about it.

'But they will be sorry,' he said. 'I could tell them where to look for the escaped prisoner, but I am not going to help them. You see, I have been searching the moors with my telescope, and although I have not actually seen the prisoner, I *have* seen the person who is taking him food.'

I thought of Barrymore and Mrs Barrymore's worried face. But Mr Frankland's next words showed me that I did not need to worry.

'You will be surprised to hear that a young boy takes food to the prisoner. The boy goes by at about the same time each day, and he is always carrying a bag. Who else can he be going to see – except the prisoner? Come and look through my telescope, and you will see that I am right. It is about this time each day that the boy goes by.'

We went up on to the roof, and we did not have to wait long. There was someone moving on a hill in front of the house. I looked through the telescope and saw a small boy with a bag over his shoulder. He looked round to make sure that nobody was following him, and then he disappeared over the hill.

'Remember that I don't want the police to know my secret, Dr Watson,' Frankland reminded me. 'I'm too angry with them at the moment to help them.'

I agreed not to tell the police, and said goodbye. I walked along the road while Frankland was watching me, but as soon as I was round the corner, I went towards the hill where we had seen the boy.

The sun was already going down when I reached the top of the hill. I could not see the boy, and there was nothing else in that lonely place. Beneath me on the other side of the hill was a circle of old stone huts. In the middle of the circle was one hut that had a better roof than the others, so it would keep out the wind and the rain. This must be the place where the mysterious man was hiding! I would soon know his secret.

As I walked towards the hut, I saw that someone had certainly been using it. A path had been worn up to the door. I took my revolver out of my pocket, and checked that it was ready to fire. I walked quickly and quietly up to the hut, and looked inside. The place was empty.

But this was certainly where the man lived. As I looked round the hut, I knew that the mysterious man must have a very strong character. No other person could live in conditions as bad as these. There were some blankets on a flat stone where the man slept. There had been a fire in one corner. There were some cooking pots, and a large bowl half full of water. In the middle of the hut was another large flat stone which was used as a table, and on it was the bag the boy had been carrying. Under the bag I saw a piece of paper with writing on it. Quickly, I picked up the paper and read what was written on it. It said: 'Dr Watson has gone to Newtown.'

I realized that the mysterious man had told someone to watch me, and this was a message from his spy. Was the man a dangerous enemy? Or was he a friend who was watching us to make sure we were safe? I decided I would not leave the hut until I knew.

Outside, the sun was low in the sky. Everything looked

calm and peaceful in the golden evening light. But I did not feel peaceful or calm. I felt frightened as I waited for the mysterious man.

Then I heard footsteps coming towards the hut. As they came closer, I moved into the darkest corner of the hut. I did not want the man to see me until I had looked closely at him. The footsteps stopped, and I could hear nothing at all. Then the man began to move again, and the footsteps came closer. A shadow fell across the door of the hut.

'It's a lovely evening, my dear Watson,' said a voice I knew well. 'I really think you will enjoy it more out here.'

13

Too Late

For a moment or two I could neither breathe nor move. Then I felt my fear and unhappiness disappear, as I knew that I was no longer alone in my responsibility for Sir Henry. The dangers all around me did not seem so frightening. The cool voice could belong to only one man in the world.

'Holmes!' I cried. 'Holmes!'

I went outside the hut, and there was Holmes. He was sitting on a stone, and his grey eyes were dancing with amusement. He was thin and worn, but bright and wide-awake. His skin was brown from the wind and the sun.

I went outside the hut, and there was Holmes.

But his chin was smooth, and his shirt was white. He did not look like a man who had been living in the middle of the moor.

'I have never been so glad to see anyone in my life,' I said, 'nor so surprised.'

'I am surprised, too,' Holmes said, as he shook me warmly by the hand. 'How did you find me?'

I told him about Frankland, and how I had seen the boy with the food.

Holmes went into the hut, and looked at the food, and at the note with it. 'I guess that you have been to see Mrs Laura Lyons,' he said, and when I told him that he was right, he went on: 'When we put together everything that each of us has discovered, I expect we shall know almost everything about this case.'

'But how did you get here?' I asked him. 'And what have you been doing? I thought you had to finish your case in London.'

'That is what I wanted you to think,' he said.

'Then you have tricked me, and have no confidence in me,' I said. I was upset and angry because he had not told me his plans.

'I am sorry if it seems I have tricked you, my dear Watson. I did not want our enemy to know I was here, but I wanted to be near enough to make sure that you and Sir Henry were safe. You are a kind person – too kind to leave me alone out here in bad weather. Our enemy would guess I was here if he saw you coming out with food, or with important news. You have been a very real help to me. Your letters with all their valuable information have been brought to me. You have done excellent work, and without you I would not have all the important details I needed.'

Holmes' warm words of thanks made me feel much happier, and I saw that he was right.

'That's better,' he said, as he saw the shadow lift from my face. 'Now tell me about your visit to Mrs Laura Lyons.'

I told Holmes everything Mrs Lyons had said.

'This is all very important,' Holmes said. 'It answers questions I have been unable to answer. Did you know that Mrs Lyons and Stapleton are very close friends? They often meet, and they write to each other. Perhaps I can use this information to turn Stapleton's wife against him . . .'

'His wife?' I asked. 'Who and where is she?'

'The lady called Miss Stapleton, who pretends to be his sister, is really his wife,' said Holmes.

'Good heavens, Holmes! Are you sure? If she is his wife, why did Stapleton allow Sir Henry to fall in love with her?'

'Sir Henry hurt nobody except himself when he fell in love with her. Stapleton took care that Sir Henry did not *make* love to her. I repeat that the lady is his wife, and not his sister. They came here only two years ago, and before that he owned a school in the north of England. He told you that, and you told me in your letter. I checked on the school, and found that the man who had owned it went away with his wife when the school closed. They changed their name, but the couple who were described to me were without doubt the Stapletons.'

'But why do they pretend to be brother and sister?' I asked.

'Because Stapleton thought that she would be very much more useful to him if she appeared to be a free woman.'

Suddenly I saw behind Stapleton's smiling face a heart with murder in it. 'So *he* is our enemy! *He* is the man who followed us in London! And the warning note to Sir Henry came from Miss Stapleton.'

'Exactly,' said Holmes.

'But if Miss Stapleton is really his wife, why is he a close friend of Mrs Laura Lyons?'

'Your excellent work has given us the answer to that question, Watson. When you told me that Mrs Lyons was getting a divorce, I realized that she hoped to marry Stapleton. He told her that he was unmarried, and that he wanted to make her his wife. When she learns the truth, she may decide to help us. We must go and see her tomorrow.'

'One last question, Holmes,' I said. 'What is Stapleton trying to do?'

Holmes dropped his voice as he answered: 'Murder, cold-blooded murder. That is what Stapleton is trying to do. Do not ask me for details. I am about to catch him in a trap. There is only one danger – that he will act before I am ready. Another day, or perhaps two, and I shall complete my case. Until then you must guard Sir Henry very closely. You should be with him today. However, what you have discovered is very valuable.'

59

As he finished speaking, an awful scream – a long cry of pain and horror – broke the silence of the moor. The sound turned my blood to ice.

'Oh, my God,' I whispered. 'What is that?'

Holmes had jumped to his feet. 'Where is it, Watson?' he whispered, and I could see that he was shaken by the scream.

The hopeless cry came again, louder, nearer, and more terrible than before. With it came a new sound – deep and frightening.

'The hound!' cried Holmes. 'Come, Watson, come! Great heavens! If we are too late . . .'

14

Death on the Moor

Holmes started running over the moor, and I followed him. From somewhere in front of us came one more hopeless scream. It was followed by the sound of something falling heavily. We stopped and listened.

I saw Holmes put his hand to his head. 'He has won, Watson. We're too late. I was mad not to act sooner. And you, Watson, look what happens when you leave the man I asked you to guard. But if the worst has happened, we shall see that Stapleton doesn't go free.'

We ran through the dark towards the place where the cries had come from. We reached a rocky edge from which a steep side fell away. Below us we saw the body of a man. He was lying with his face down on the ground. He had fallen on his head, which was bent under him, and his neck was broken. Holmes lit a match. We saw with horror the blood running out on to the ground from his head.

We both remembered clearly the suit the man was wearing. It was a thick, red-brown country suit. It was the suit Sir Henry had been wearing on the morning when we first met him in Baker Street. We saw it for a moment and then the match went out. Our hearts turned sick and cold inside us.

'The devil! The murderer! I shall never forgive myself for leaving Sir Henry alone,' I whispered angrily.

'It's more my fault than yours,' said Holmes. 'I have let this good man die because I was busy with the last details of my case. It is the greatest mistake I have ever made. But why did he come out on to the moor? I told him it would lead to his death. Now both Sir Henry and his uncle have been murdered. By heavens, clever as he is, I shall trap Stapleton before another day is past.'

With heavy hearts we stood on either side of the broken body. Then Holmes bent over the body and began to move it. All of a sudden he began to laugh and jump up and down.

'Look at the face!' he shouted, hitting me on the back. 'It is not Sir Henry. It's Selden, the escaped prisoner.'

We turned the body over. There was no doubt about it. I had seen the face before, on the night Sir Henry and

61

*We saw with horror the blood running out on to the ground
from his head.*

I had chased Selden over the moor. Then I suddenly remembered, and everything became clear. Sir Henry had told me how he gave his old clothes to Barrymore. I realized that this suit had been among the clothes Barrymore had left for Selden, and I told Holmes.

'Then the clothes have caused the death of the poor man. The hound had been given something of Sir Henry's to smell so that it would pick up his scent and follow him. I think that is why the shoe was taken from the hotel in London. So the hound followed the scent and hunted this man. But there is one thing I don't understand. How did Selden know that the hound was following him? We know he ran a long way. He was screaming for a long time before he fell, and we could hear that he was running as he screamed. So the hound was a long way behind him when he began to run. How could he see it in the dark? How did he know it was there, until it was close behind him?'

'I cannot answer that,' I said, 'but there is something else I don't understand. Why was the hound out on the moor tonight? Stapleton would not let it go out unless he thought Sir Henry was there.'

'We may know the answer to that question very soon,' said Holmes. 'Here comes Stapleton.'

His sharp eyes had seen a figure moving in the darkness in front of us, and as the man came closer, I could see that it was indeed Stapleton.

'We must be very careful not to show that we suspect him,' Holmes warned me.

Stapleton stopped when he saw us, and then walked forward again. 'Dr Watson, is that you? I didn't expect to see you on the moor at this time of night. But, dear me, what's this? Somebody hurt? Not – don't tell me that it's our friend Sir Henry!'

He went past me and bent over the dead man. I heard him breathe in quickly.

'Who . . . who is this?' he asked, his voice shaking.

'It's Selden, the escaped prisoner.'

Stapleton quickly managed to hide the look of surprise and disappointment on his face as he turned towards us. He looked sharply from Holmes to me. 'Dear me! How terrible! How did he die?'

'We think he broke his neck by falling over the edge of these rocks,' I said.

'I heard a cry, and that is why I came out. I was worried about Sir Henry,' Stapleton said.

'Why were you worried about Sir Henry?' I asked.

'Because I had invited him to my house. When he did not come I was surprised. Then, when I heard cries on the moor, I began to worry about him. I wonder' – his eyes went quickly from my face to Holmes' – 'did you hear anything else at all?'

'No,' said Holmes. 'Did you?'

'No,' said Stapleton.

'What do you mean, then?'

'Oh, you know the stories about the supernatural hound. I wondered if it had been here tonight.'

'We heard nothing of that kind,' I said.

'How do you think this poor man fell to his death?' Stapleton asked.

'I think cold and hunger, and his fear that the police would catch him, drove him mad. He ran round the moor in his madness, and fell over this edge,' I said.

'Do you agree, Mr Sherlock Holmes?' asked Stapleton.

'You're quick to guess who I am,' said Holmes.

'We've been expecting you ever since Dr Watson arrived.'

'I have no doubt my friend is right about the way Selden died,' said Holmes. 'It's a sad death, but it will not prevent me from returning to London tomorrow.'

'Before you return, will you be able to explain the mysteries that we've experienced here?'

'I am not always as successful as I hope. I need facts, not stories of the supernatural. This hasn't been a good case for me.'

Stapleton looked hard at him, but Holmes had spoken very seriously and his words sounded true.

We covered the body. Then Stapleton turned to go home, and Holmes and I walked towards Baskerville Hall.

'He's a very clever man, and a dangerous enemy, who will be difficult to trap,' said Holmes. 'Look how he controlled his disappointment when he found that the dead man was not Sir Henry.'

'I'm sorry that he has seen you,' I said.

'So am I, but there was nothing we could do about it.

Now he knows I am here he may be more careful, or he may act more quickly than he had planned.'

'Why can't we give him to the police at once?'

'Because we can't prove anything against him. Sir Charles was found dead because his heart failed. Again, tonight we could not prove that there was a hound. Selden died from a fall. We have no case at present. We shall see Mrs Lyons tomorrow, and she may help us. But whatever happens, I have my own plan. There will be some danger, but by the end of tomorrow I hope to have won this battle.'

He would say nothing else.

'Are you coming to the Hall?' I asked.

'Yes,' he replied. 'There is no reason for me to hide any longer. But one last word, Watson. Say nothing of the hound to Sir Henry. Let him think that Selden died from a fall. If he knows about the hound, he will find it harder to face the dangers of tomorrow. I think you told me in your last letter that he is having dinner with the Stapletons tomorrow evening.'

'And they have invited me, too,' I reminded him.

'Then you must excuse yourself, and he must go alone. That can easily be arranged. And now I think we are both ready for some food.'

15

The Trap

When we reached the Hall, Sir Henry was very pleased to see Holmes. But he was surprised that Holmes had no luggage and that he appeared so unexpectedly.

I had the unhappy job of telling Barrymore and his wife about her brother's death. Mrs Barrymore cried and was very sad indeed.

During dinner Sir Henry told us that he had spent a dull day and evening on his own. He had kept his promise to Holmes, and so he had not accepted the Stapleton's invitation to their house that evening. We did not tell him how glad we were that he had stayed away from the moor!

Holmes started to say something, and then he stopped suddenly. His eyes were fixed on one of the pictures of the past Baskervilles on the wall.

'Sir Henry, could you tell me which Baskerville that is?' he asked. Sir Henry and I both looked at the picture.

'That is Sir Hugo, the one who started all the trouble,' said Sir Henry. 'He was the first to see the Hound.'

Holmes looked hard at the picture, but said nothing more.

Then after Sir Henry had gone to his room, Holmes made me stand in front of the picture. 'Is it like anyone you know?' he asked. He stood on a chair, and with his hands he covered the hat and hair of the man in the picture.

'Is the face like anyone you know?' Holmes asked.

'Good heavens!' I cried in surprise. I was looking at a picture of Stapleton's face.

'Yes,' said Holmes before I could say anything more. 'There's not much doubt about it. Stapleton is a Baskerville. He looks like Sir Hugo, and he has the same evil character. Now I understand why he wants to kill Sir Henry. I am sure we shall find that he will inherit the Baskerville lands. And so we have one more answer. By tomorrow night Stapleton will be caught like one of his butterflies, and we shall add him to the Baker Street collection.'

We soon went to bed. I was up early in the morning, but Holmes was up earlier. He had already sent one message to the police about Selden, and another to his boy to stop him taking food to the hut.

When Sir Henry joined us, Holmes told him that we had to leave for London immediately after breakfast. Sir Henry was very unhappy about this, but Holmes asked him to help us by doing everything Holmes ordered him to do. Sir Henry agreed to help in this way, and to go by himself to the Stapletons that evening. He also agreed to tell the Stapletons that Holmes and I had gone to London, but that we would return to Devonshire soon.

'One more order,' said Holmes. 'I want you to drive to the Stapletons' house and then send the driver away. Let the Stapletons know that you're going to walk home across the moor.'

'Across the moor?' said Sir Henry, very surprised. 'But you have told me again and again not to do that.'

'This time it will be completely safe. I know that you are brave enough to do it, and it *must* be done.'

'Then I will do it.'

'But you *must* keep to the path between the Stapletons' house and the Grimpen road, which is your natural way home. Do not leave the path and the road.'

I was very surprised by all this. Holmes had told Stapleton that he would return to London, but he had not said that I was going too. And I was very worried that neither of us would be with Sir Henry when he walked across the moor that night. But we had to obey Holmes' orders.

Holmes and I left Baskerville Hall immediately after breakfast and went to the station at Newtown. A small boy was waiting on the platform.

'Any orders, sir?' he asked Holmes.

'You will take the train to London, my boy. When you get there, you will send a telegram to Sir Henry in my name. It will ask him to send to me at Baker Street the pocket book I left at the Hall.'

I began to understand some of Holmes' plan. When Sir Henry received the telegram sent by Holmes' boy, he would think that we had arrived in London. He would tell Stapleton, who would then also believe that we were far away from Baskerville Hall. In fact, we would be very close in case Sir Henry needed us.

We left the station and went to see Mrs Laura Lyons. I introduced Holmes to her. After they had shaken hands, he said: 'Dr Watson has told me everything, Mrs Lyons. We see Sir Charles' death as a case of murder. Both Stapleton and his wife are suspects.'

Mrs Lyons jumped from her chair. 'His wife!' she cried. 'He has no wife. He is not a married man.'

'I have come here ready to prove that he is married, and the woman who calls herself his sister is really his wife,' said Holmes. He took some photographs and papers from his pocket, and showed them to Mrs Lyons. She looked at the photographs and read the papers. When she put them down, I could see that she had accepted the truth.

'I thought this man loved me,' she said, 'but he has lied to me. Ask me what you like, Mr Holmes, and I will tell you the truth. I never thought any harm would come to Sir Charles. He was a dear old gentleman who was very kind to me. I would do nothing to hurt him.'

'I believe you, Mrs Lyons,' said Holmes. 'Now, let me tell you what I think happened. You can tell me if I'm right or if I'm wrong. First of all, I think Stapleton told you to write the letter to Sir Charles and to ask him for help. He also told you to ask Sir Charles to meet you at the moor gate. Then, after you had sent the letter, Stapleton persuaded you not to meet Sir Charles after all.'

'Stapleton told me that he could not allow any other man to give me the money for my divorce,' Mrs Lyons said. 'He said he was poor, but that he would give all his money to bring us together. Then, after I heard about Sir

71

Charles' death, Stapleton told me to say nothing about my letter and the meeting. He said I would be a suspect. He frightened me into staying silent.'

'Yes,' said Holmes. 'But you wondered about him?'

She said nothing for a moment, and looked down. 'Yes,' she said. 'But since he has lied to me about marrying me, I will no longer keep his secrets.'

'You are lucky that you have escaped him,' Holmes said. 'You know too much. But I hope you are safe now. Good morning, Mrs Lyons, and thank you. You will hear from us soon.'

'So one by one our questions are answered,' said Holmes as we left Newtown. 'When it is over, this will be one of the most famous cases of our time. And now it has nearly ended. We must hope that it ends safely and successfully.'

16

The Hound of the Baskervilles

That evening Holmes and I drove across the moor until we could see the lights of the Stapletons' house in front of us. Then we got out and began to walk very quietly along the path towards the house. When we were very close, Holmes told me to stop. He took his revolver from his pocket, and I did the same.

'We shall hide behind these rocks,' he whispered. 'Watson, you know the house, so I want you to go forward and look through the windows. I want to know where the Stapletons and Sir Henry are, and what they are doing. Take great care, because they must not know that somebody is watching them.'

Very carefully and quietly I moved towards the house. I looked first into the dining-room window. Stapleton and Sir Henry were sitting and smoking their cigars, but there was no sign of Miss Stapleton. I moved round to the other windows, but I could not see her in any of the rooms.

I went back to the dining-room window, and as I looked in again, Stapleton left the room and came out of the house. He went to a hut beside the house, and unlocked the door. I heard a strange sound coming from the hut, but I could not think what was making the noise. Then Stapleton locked the door, and went back into the house and into the dining room.

I went back to Holmes and told him what I had seen. He wanted to know where Miss Stapleton was, and I had to tell him twice that there was no sign of her in the house.

The moon was shining on the Great Grimpen Marsh, and a fog was rising from it. Holmes watched the fog and began to look worried. The fog was creeping up from the marsh towards the house. We were hidden near the path, which was on the far side of the house from the marsh.

'The fog is moving towards us, Watson, and that is very serious,' said Holmes. 'It is the one thing that could make my plans go wrong.'

As we watched, the fog, which had crept as far as the

house, began to flow round it. Angrily Holmes hit the rock in front of us with his open hand.

'If Sir Henry doesn't come out in the next quarter of an hour, the path will be covered by the fog. In half an hour we shall not be able to see our hands in front of our faces. We must move back to higher ground above the fog.'

We moved away from the house and out of the fog, which was creeping slowly along the ground and hiding the path from our view.

'We must not go too far,' said Holmes. 'If we do, Sir Henry may be caught before he reaches us.'

Holmes went down on one knee, and put his ear to the ground. 'Thank heaven, I think I hear him coming.'

Then we heard quick footsteps on the path. After a few moments, Sir Henry appeared out of the fog and walked on in the clear moonlight. He came quickly along the path, passed close to where we were hidden, and began to walk up the hill behind us. As he walked, he looked over his shoulder again and again, like a man who is worried that something is following him.

'Listen!' said Holmes sharply. 'Look out! It's coming!'

I heard him make his revolver ready to fire, and I did the same.

There was a sound of quick, light footsteps from inside the curtain of fog. The thick cloud had crept to within fifty metres of where we were hidden. We tried to see into it, and wondered what horrible thing would appear. I looked at Holmes. His eyes were fixed on the place where the path disappeared into the fog. He was pale, but his eyes were bright. He looked like a man who was going to win the most important game of his life. Then suddenly his eyes nearly jumped out of his head, and his mouth opened in frightened surprise. I looked away from him to see what his eyes were fixed on. When I saw the awful shape that was coming towards us out of the fog, my blood turned cold. The revolver nearly fell from my hands, and my whole body froze with fear.

I saw a hound, an enormous black hound. It was bigger than any dog I had ever seen. But it was something else that filled us with terror. No human eye had ever seen a hound like this one. Fire came from its open mouth. Its eyes were burning. Flames covered its head and body. It was a more horrible sight than anyone could imagine – a hell-hound sent by the devil. It was not a creature of the natural world.

The huge, black, burning hound ran quickly and silently after Sir Henry. Far away along the path we saw him turn and look back at the hound. His face was white in the moonlight and his hands were lifted in horror. He watched helplessly as the terrible creature got closer to him. We were so frozen by the ghostly and unnatural sight that we let the hound go past us, and we could not move. Our friend was near to death, and we were helpless with fear.

17

The Search for the Murderer

Then our fear for Sir Henry became greater than our terror. Holmes and I fired our revolvers together. The creature gave a loud cry of pain, and we knew we had hit it. But it did not stop, and ran on, after Sir Henry.

When we heard the cry of pain, our fears disappeared. This was no supernatural hound. Our bullets could hurt it, and we could kill it. We ran after it as fast as we could. I have never seen anyone run as quickly as Holmes ran that night, and I could not keep up with him. In front of us on the path we heard scream after scream from Sir Henry, and the deep voice of the hound. I saw the creature jump at Sir Henry and throw him to the ground. Its teeth went for his throat. But the next moment Holmes had emptied his revolver into the hound's body. It gave a last deep cry, its teeth closed on the empty air, and it fell to the ground. I put my revolver to its head, but I did not need to fire. The hound was dead.

Sir Henry lay unconscious where he had fallen. Quickly we opened the neck of his shirt. Holmes had fired just in time, and the hound's teeth had not reached our friend's throat. Already his eyes were beginning to open and he looked up at us.

'My God,' he whispered. 'What was it? What in heaven's name was it?'

Holmes emptied his revolver into the hound's body.

'It's dead, whatever it was,' said Holmes. 'We've killed the family ghost for ever.'

The creature that lay before us was as large as a small lion. Its mouth and teeth were huge. They shone with blue flames. There were rings of blue fire round its cruel eyes, too. I touched the hound's burning coat. When I held up my hand, it, too, seemed to be on fire.

'Phosphorus,' I said. 'That is why the hound appears to burn in the dark. Stapleton put phosphorus paint on the hound in the hut beside the house.'

But Holmes was thinking more about Sir Henry than about Stapleton's cleverness.

'I must apologize to you, Sir Henry,' he said. 'I put your life in danger. I expected to see a huge hound, but not a creature like this. The fog gave us a very short time to control our fear, and for moments we could not move.'

'Never mind,' said Sir Henry. 'You saved my life, and I thank you. Please help me stand up. What are you going to do now?'

Sir Henry's legs were shaking so much from his terrible experience that he could not stand. We helped him to a rock. He sat there and held his head in his hands.

'We must leave you here, Sir Henry, and try to catch Stapleton. We shall come back as quickly as possible and take you to the Hall. Our case is complete, but we must now catch our man.'

I followed Holmes along the path back to the house.

'We must search the house,' said Holmes, 'but almost

certainly he won't be there. He probably heard the noise of our guns, so he knows his evil game is finished.'

The front door of the house was open. We went in and looked from room to room. All the rooms downstairs were empty, so we went upstairs and looked in all the rooms except one, which was locked.

'There's someone in there,' I said. 'I heard someone move. Help me break open this door.'

We threw ourselves against the door, and as the lock broke we went in. We held our revolvers ready to fire.

In the middle of the room was a figure tied to a post. We could not see whether it was a man or a woman, as it was completely covered with sheets. Only the eyes and nose were free.

We pulled off the sheets and untied the prisoner from the post. It was Miss Stapleton. As we untied her, we could see long red bruises across her neck.

'That cruel devil Stapleton has beaten her,' Holmes said. 'Put her into a chair.' Miss Stapleton had fainted from the beating and exhaustion. As we put her into the chair, she opened her eyes.

'Is he safe?' she asked. 'Has he escaped?'

'He cannot escape us, Miss Stapleton,' Holmes said.

'No, no, I don't mean my husband. I mean Sir Henry. Is he safe?'

'Yes,' I said, 'and the hound is dead.'

'Thank God,' she said. 'Thank God. Oh, the cruel devil. Look what he has done to me.' She showed us her arms, and we saw with horror that her skin was black and blue where she had been beaten. 'But he has hurt me more in other ways. While I thought he loved me, I accepted many things. But he doesn't love me. He has used me.'

'Then help us now,' said Holmes. 'Tell us where he has gone.'

'There is an old house on an island in the middle of the marsh,' she said. 'He kept his hound there. He also had the house ready in case he needed to escape. He will be there, I'm sure.'

'Nobody could find his way into the Grimpen Marsh in this fog tonight,' said Holmes, looking out of the window.

The fog lay like white wool against the glass, and we knew we could not try to follow him until it cleared. We decided to take Sir Henry back to Baskerville Hall. We had to tell him everything about the Stapletons, and he was deeply hurt when he heard the truth about the woman he loved. The news that she was married, and the awful fear he had experienced, brought on a fever. We sent for Dr Mortimer, who came and sat with Sir Henry throughout the night.

On the following morning Miss Stapleton took us to the path through the marsh. The fog had lifted, and she showed us the sticks which she and her husband had put in to mark the way. We followed them through the marsh, which smelled of dying plants. The wet ground pulled at our feet as we walked. From time to time one of us stepped from the path and sank up to his waist in the marsh. One man on his own could not hope to escape the pull of the marsh; without help he would sink to his death.

But we did not find any sign of Stapleton. We searched and searched without success. There is no doubt that he lost his way in the fog, and sank in the marsh. Somewhere, deep down, his body lies to this day.

We reached the island Miss Stapleton had described, and searched the old house.

'This place tells us nothing that we do not already know,' said Holmes. 'These bones show that he hid the hound here, but he could not keep it quiet, so people heard its cries. Here is the bottle of phosphorus paint. Stapleton used it very cleverly on the hound. After what we saw and felt last night, we cannot be surprised that Sir Charles died of fright. And now I understand how Selden knew that the hound was following him in the dark. It's not surprising the poor man screamed and ran as he did. The old story of the supernatural hound probably gave Stapleton the idea of using phosphorus. Very clever. I said it in London and I say it again, Watson. We have never had a more dangerous enemy than the one who is lying out there' – and he pointed to the great marsh that was all round us.

18

Looking Back

It was the end of November, more than a month after our return from Baskerville Hall. Holmes and I were sitting on either side of a bright fire in our sitting room in Baker Street. Since our return, Holmes had been working hard on two other cases, and he had been too busy to discuss the Baskerville case. But now the other cases were finished, and he had been successful in both of them. I decided it was a good time to ask him the final questions about Stapleton and the hound.

'The picture showed us that Stapleton was indeed a Baskerville,' Holmes began. 'He was the son of Roger Baskerville, who was Sir Charles' younger brother. Roger was a criminal who escaped from prison and ran away to South America. Everyone thought he had died unmarried, but that was not true. He had one son, also called Roger, whom we knew as Stapleton. Stapleton married a beautiful South American, and came to England, where he started a school in the north. He discovered that he would inherit the Baskerville lands and fortune if Sir Charles and Sir Henry both died. That is why he moved to Devonshire when the school closed.

'When he met Sir Charles, he heard the story of the hell-hound. He also learned that Sir Charles believed these supernatural stories, and that he had a weak heart.

82

I had one last question for Holmes.

'Stapleton had the idea of buying a huge hound, and of using the phosphorus to make it shine like the hound in the story. I have found the place where he bought the animal. He took it by train to Devonshire and walked many miles over the moors with it so that it would not be seen near Baskerville Hall.

'He needed to get Sir Charles out of the Hall at night. This would be easy to do if his wife made Sir Charles fall in love with her. But, although he beat her, she refused to help him with his evil plan.

'Then Stapleton met Laura Lyons. We know that he made her write a letter to bring Sir Charles to the moor gate on that sad night. The hound, which was shining with phosphorus, chased Sir Charles down the Yew Alley. Sir Charles' terror was so great that his weak heart stopped, and he died, but the animal did not touch the dead body.

'The hound had run on the grass, so it left no footprints, except the one found by Dr Mortimer. You see how clever Stapleton was. Neither he nor the hound had touched Sir Charles so there was no sign of murder. The only two people who might suspect him – his wife and Mrs Lyons – could not be certain about what he had done. Anyway, neither of them would inform the police about him.

'Next, Stapleton learned that Sir Henry had reached England, so he went to London. He hoped to murder Sir Henry there. He took his wife with him, but he wasn't sure that she would keep his secret, so he did not tell her the truth. He locked her up in their hotel. She knew that he had some evil plan, but she was too frightened to give Sir Henry a clear warning. Instead, she sent him the letter made of words cut from a newspaper.

'Meanwhile, Stapleton was wearing a false beard and following Sir Henry. He needed something to give the hound Sir Henry's scent, so he paid a maid at Sir Henry's hotel to steal one of his shoes. The first one was a new one, and didn't have Sir Henry's scent on it. It was no use for the hound, so he put it back, and another, older, shoe was stolen. When the shoes were changed, I knew that the hound must be a natural and not a supernatural creature.

'Next there was the letter made of words cut from a newspaper. When I looked at it, I held it close to my eyes. I noticed a smell of perfume, so I guessed that a woman had sent the letter.

'By the time I went to Devonshire I knew that there was a real hound, and I knew we were looking for a man and a woman. I guessed that the Stapletons were the pair. I had to watch Stapleton, but I had to hide myself. As I have explained, I could not tell you what I was doing. I stayed in Newtown and used the hut on the moor only when necessary.

'Your letters were sent to me immediately from Baker Street, and were very helpful. When you told me that Stapleton had owned a school in the north of England, I checked on him and where he had come from. I discovered he had come from South America. And then everything became clear.

'By the time you found me on the moor, I knew everything, but I could prove nothing. We had to catch the man doing something criminal, and so I had to put Sir Henry in danger.

'Dr Mortimer tells me that Sir Henry will be completely better after some rest. As you know, the two of them have become good friends, and are going on a long holiday together. Sir Henry will take some time to forget Miss Stapleton. He loved her deeply and it hurt him badly when he learned the truth about her.

'She was very frightened of her cruel husband, but she suspected that he was responsible for Sir Charles' death. She knew about the hound, and when Selden died she guessed that the hound had killed him. She knew her husband had the hound at their house on the night Sir Henry came to dinner. They argued about the hound that evening, and as they argued Stapleton told her about Mrs Lyons. Any love she had for her husband disappeared at that moment. He knew that she wanted to help Sir Henry, so he beat her and tied her up.

'He probably hoped that when he inherited the Baskerville lands, she would love him again. He certainly thought that she would keep silent if she became Lady Baskerville. But I think he was wrong. He had been too cruel to her. She could not forgive him or love him again, nor, I think, allow him to enjoy the results of his crime.

'Of course, he could not frighten Sir Henry in the same way as Sir Charles. Sir Henry was a young and healthy man. So he kept the hound hungry. He knew that the animal would either kill Sir Henry or would hurt him so badly that it would be easy to complete the murder.'

I had one last question for Holmes. 'But Stapleton was living so close to Baskerville Hall and using a false name. It looked very strange. How would he explain that to the police, if after Sir Henry's death he then inherited the Baskerville lands and fortune?'

'I don't know how he planned to explain the false name and why he was living at Pen House,' said Holmes. 'I can only say that he was a very clever man. I am sure he had thought of an answer to the problem.

'But that's enough work for the evening, Watson. I have two tickets for the theatre. If we get ready now, we shall have time to stop at my favourite restaurant for some dinner on the way.'

GLOSSARY

alley   a narrow road or path

ash   powder that is left after something has been burnt

butler   a man servant (a person who works in someone else's house)

butterfly   an insect with large white or coloured wings

case   something (a problem or a crime) investigated by the police

cheerful   happy

cigar   a longer, thicker, brown 'cigarette'

county   a large area of a country, e.g. Britain is divided into many counties

creature   a living animal or person

creep (past tense **crept**)   to move slowly along close to the ground

devil   a cruel or evil person

Devil (the)   the strongest evil spirit (Satan), and the enemy of God

divorce *(n)*   the end of a marriage by law

enormous   very big; huge

evil   very bad; harmful

faint *(v)*   to become unconscious for a short time

fire *(v)*   to shoot a gun

footprint   a mark on the ground made by a foot or shoe

forgive   to stop being angry with someone about something

grim   (of a place) frightening and unwelcoming

heaven(s)   the place where God is believed to live; often used in expressions of surprise or fear, e.g. *Good heavens, Great heavens*

hedge *(n)* a row of small trees planted close together

hell the place where the devil is believed to live, and where bad people are punished after they die

horrible frightening, terrible; causing horror

hound *(n)* a kind of dog used for chasing, catching and sometimes killing wild animals

huge very big; enormous

hunt *(v)* to chase wild animals, and try to catch or kill them

hut a small building made of stone or wood, with one room

ink a black or coloured liquid used for writing

ivy a climbing plant with shiny, dark green leaves

lion a large, dangerous wild animal of the 'cat' family

maid a woman servant

mark *(v)* to put some kind of sign on something

marsh very wet, soft ground

moor open, rough, windy land, usually on hills and without trees

net something made of pieces of string (or wire) joined together; used for catching insects, fish, etc.

pale not bright; with a light or weak colour

perfume a liquid with a sweet smell to put on the body

phosphorus a chemical material which shines in the dark and appears to burn

print *(n)* a mark made by something pressing on something else (e.g. footprints)

revolver a small gun, which is held in the hand

scent *(n)* the smell of an animal or a person, which another animal (e.g. a dog) can follow

science the study of natural things; biology, chemistry, physics, mathematics are sciences

sink (past tense **sank**) to go down under water (or a marsh)

supernatural *(adj)* that cannot be explained by the laws of
nature (e.g. ghosts and spirits)

tear out (past tense **tore**) to pull something out very quickly
and roughly

telegram a message sent by electric wires and then written
down

telescope a long instrument with special glass that makes
distant things (e.g. stars) look bigger and closer

terror very great fear

throat the front of the neck

trick *(v)* to do something that is not honest in order to get what
you want from somebody

upset *(adj)* unhappy or worried about something

violin a musical instrument with strings, held under the chin

waste *(v)* to spend or use something (e.g. time) in a useless way

will *(n)* somebody's written wishes that say who will inherit
their money, house, lands, etc. after they die

yew a kind of tree with small leaves that are always dark green

The Hound of the Baskervilles

ACTIVITIES

Before Reading

1 **Read the back cover and the story introduction on the first page of the book. How much do you know now about this story? Choose the best words to complete this passage.**

Dartmoor is a *real / imaginary* place in England. It is easy to *find / lose* your way on this wild, *dry / wet* moor, and there are dangerous *marshes / rocks* covered in *black / green* plants, which hide the *soft / hard* earth underneath. The weather can change very *slowly / suddenly*, from a *dark / clear* sky to a thick *mist / cloud*. Once, a huge hound lived there – a *dog / cat* from *heaven / hell*, that brought a *horrible / pleasant* death to all who saw it. Only the great *spy / detective*, Sherlock Holmes, could *cause / solve* the mystery of this hound.

2 **Can you guess what will happen in this story? Choose some answers to these questions.**

1 Will anybody die in this story? If so, will it be . . .
   a) an escaped prisoner?   c) a man called Baskerville?
   b) Sherlock Holmes?   d) a murderer?

2 If there is a death, will it be . . .
   a) a murder?   c) from natural causes?
   b) a death by drowning?   d) an accident?

3 Will the Hound of the Baskervilles be . . .
   a) a real dog?   c) another kind of animal?
   b) a supernatural dog?   d) somebody's bad dream?

While Reading

Read Chapters 1 to 4. What do you know about the case so far? Decide which of these statements are facts, and which are guesses. Explain why you think this.

1 Sir Charles Baskerville was murdered.
2 Sir Charles walked to the gate in Yew Alley, but then ran to the end of the Alley.
3 He had stood at the gate in Yew Alley for some minutes.
4 He was expecting to meet someone at the moor gate.
5 There was a large dog in the Alley that night.
6 Sir Charles's death was caused by his weak heart.
7 The Hound of the Baskervilles sent Sir Charles mad with fear, which caused his heart to fail.

Read Chapters 5 to 8, and answer these questions.

1 Five mysterious things happened to Sir Henry before he left London. What were they?
2 Sir Henry had two uncles. What happened to them?
3 Who was Selden, and why were people frightened of him?
4 How did Dr Watson know that Barrymore was lying?
5 Holmes had a clever idea to prove that Barrymore was *not* the man in the taxi. Why didn't it work?
6 Two mysterious things happened when Dr Watson met the Stapletons on the moor. What were they?

Before you read Chapter 9, which of these statements do you agree or disagree with, and why?

1 There really is a dangerous hound on the moor.
2 Sir Henry's life is in danger from a person, not a dog.
3 The danger will probably come from Barrymore.
4 There is no reason for Sir Henry to be afraid of the Stapletons.

Read Chapters 9 to 11. What do we learn in these chapters about the following?

1 Sir Henry and Miss Stapleton
2 Barrymore, Mrs Barrymore, and Selden
3 The night Sir Charles died
4 The man on the moor who was *not* Selden
5 Mrs Laura Lyons and Sir Charles

Before you read Chapter 12, can you guess who the man on the moor is?

Read Chapters 12 to 14, and complete these two paragraphs with the right names.

Dr Watson learnt from _____ that _____ was not _____'s sister, but his wife. _____ was also very friendly with _____, who hoped to marry him. _____ planned to tell _____ that _____ was married, in the hope that she would help them.

When _____ and _____ found the body on the moor, at first they thought it was _____. Then they realized that it was _____, wearing _____'s clothes, which had been given to him by _____. The hound had been hunting _____ because of the scent on _____'s clothes. Then _____ arrived, and was clearly disappointed that the dead man was not _____.

Read Chapters 15 and 16. Who said this, and to whom? Who or what were they talking about?

1 'Is it like anyone you know?'
2 'But you have told me again and again not to do that.'
3 'He frightened me into staying silent.'
4 'They must not know that somebody is watching them.'
5 'It is the one thing that could make my plans go wrong.'
6 'Look out! It's coming!'

Before you read Chapter 17, can you guess what will happen?

1 The hound will kill Sir Henry.
2 Holmes and Watson will shoot the dog in time.
3 Stapleton will be caught and sent to prison.
4 Somebody will fall into the marsh in the fog and drown.

Read Chapters 17 and 18, and answer these questions about Stapleton's plan.

1 Why did he want to kill Sir Charles and Sir Henry?
2 What part did the phosphorus and Sir Henry's shoes play in his plan?
3 What did he make his wife and Laura Lyons do?
4 What happened to Stapleton in the end?

After Reading

1 Here is one of Dr Watson's letters to Holmes, written after his first day in Devon. Put these parts of sentences together, and join them with these linking words.

and / because / but / but / so / that / which / while / who / who / whose

Dear Holmes,

1 We arrived late yesterday evening at Baskerville Hall,

2 On the drive from the station we heard about the escape of a prisoner,

3 At the Hall we were met by the butler, Barrymore,

4 So I decided to check at the local post office

5 It hadn't. The stupid boy had given it to Barrymore's *wife*,

6 Another thing – I heard a woman crying in the night,

7 Barrymore lied when he said that it wasn't his wife,

8 Today I met the Stapletons, a brother and sister,

9 There was nothing very strange about Stapleton himself,

10 And the last thing – _____ I was talking to Stapleton,

11 Stapleton told me it was the Hound of the Baskervilles,

12 _____ has a black beard just like the man in the taxi.

13 _____ she clearly had been crying – I saw her red eyes!

14 _____ is a most grim, unwelcoming building.

15 _____ his sister warned me that Sir Henry was in danger.

16 _____ perhaps the man in the taxi *was* Barrymore after all.

17 _____ name is Selden – you'll remember the case.
18 _____ have been living near the Hall for two years.
19 _____ I know you won't believe *that*, my dear Holmes!
20 I heard a strange, deep cry coming over the moor.
21 _____ your telegram had been given to Barrymore himself.
22 _____ this morning we asked Barrymore to explain this.
Regards, Watson

2 **Here are passages from two different diaries. Find the best word to fill each gap. Then say who wrote each passage, and what was happening in the story at the time.**

_____'s DIARY: How can I prevent him from _____
poor Sir Henry? He has already _____ that horrible hound to
the hut _____ the house, and put the phosphorus _____ on it,
ready for tonight. It _____ had nothing to eat, so it _____ be
very hungry. It will tear _____ Henry's throat out . . . What
can I _____? I am sure he will beat _____ again, but I'm going
to argue _____ him one last time . . .

_____'s DIARY: I have just learnt that he _____ a
married man. The woman who _____ herself his sister is in
fact _____ wife. At first I couldn't believe _____, but then
Sherlock Holmes showed me _____ papers which proved it.
How unlucky _____ am – I never seem to choose _____ right
man. I thought this man _____ me, but he has lied to _____,
again and again. And he is _____ of murdering poor Sir
Charles, who _____ so kind to me. Well, I _____ told his
secrets now, and I _____ he will be punished.

97

3 Here is a page from Holmes' notebook. What does Holmes know or suspect about these people? Put the right names with the right notes.

Barrymore and wife / Mr Stapleton / Miss Stapleton
Laura Lyons / a supernatural hound

1 _____: in love with and hopes to marry Stapleton
2 _____: wife, but pretends to be sister
3 _____: a creature from hell taking revenge on Sir Hugo's family? – no!
4 _____: both inherited £500 from Sir Charles
5 _____: looks very like Sir Hugo – must be a Baskerville?
6 _____: trying to prevent Stapleton killing Sir Henry?
7 _____: helped Stapleton to kill Sir Charles?
8 _____: would inherit Baskerville fortune before James Desmond
9 _____: easy life when living alone at the Hall
10 _____: made to *look* supernatural by owner? – how?

4 Here is another page from Holmes' notebook, about his thoughts and the clues he has collected. Complete them in your own words.

1 The warning letter sent to Sir Henry in London smelt of perfume, so it probably _____.
2 Two of Sir Henry's shoes were stolen from the hotel, but the new, unworn one was put back because _____.
3 When the stolen shoes were changed, I knew that the hound _____.

4 The man following Sir Henry in London had a thick black beard. A beard makes someone very recognizable, so _____.

5 I shall go down to the moor and hide somewhere, in order to _____. I shan't tell Watson about this plan because he _____.

6 Stapleton used to live in the north of England, but before that he came from South America, where _____.

7 There is no proof for either the murder or the attempted murder, so I _____.

5 What did you think about this story? Do you agree (A) or disagree (D) with these ideas? Can you explain why?

1 It is easy to believe in a supernatural hound in a wild place like Dartmoor.

2 The three women in the story – Mrs Barrymore, Miss Stapleton, Laura Lyons – were all dishonest people.

3 Holmes' plan for trapping Stapleton was a very dangerous one, because it put Sir Henry's life in danger. Why didn't he just find the hound and shoot it?

6 Watson asked Holmes this question, but the great detective did not have an answer. Can *you* think of an answer?

Imagine that Stapleton's plan was successful – Sir Henry dies and Stapleton then inherits the Baskerville lands and fortune. But it would look very strange that Stapleton was living close to Baskerville Hall and using a false name. How would he explain that to the police?

ABOUT THE AUTHOR

Sir Arthur Conan Doyle (1859–1930) was born in Edinburgh, in Scotland. He studied medicine and worked as a doctor for eight years. Then he started writing in order to earn more money, and soon people were reading his stories in weekly magazines.

In the opening pages of his first novel, *A Study in Scarlet* (1887), Sherlock Holmes appeared for the first time – a strange, coldly intelligent detective, who smokes a pipe, plays the violin, and lives at 221B Baker Street in London. He can find the answer to almost any problem, and enjoys explaining how easy it is to his slow-thinking friend, Dr Watson ('Elementary, my dear Watson!'). Readers began to show great interest in Holmes when *The Sign of Four* was published in 1890, and short stories about him, in *The Strand Magazine*, were very popular.

Conan Doyle himself preferred writing novels about history, like *The White Company* (1891), and he soon became bored with the Sherlock Holmes character. So, in *The Final Problem* (1893) he killed him off, when Holmes and his famous enemy, Moriarty, fell to their deaths in the Reichenbach Falls. But because people kept asking for more stories about Holmes, Conan Doyle, rather unwillingly, had to bring him back to life, in one of his most exciting and popular stories, *The Hound of the Baskervilles* (1902).

You can read Sherlock Holmes stories in almost any language, and there are many plays and films about the great detective.

ABOUT BOOKWORMS

OXFORD BOOKWORMS LIBRARY
Classics • True Stories • Fantasy & Horror • Human Interest
Crime & Mystery • Thriller & Adventure

The OXFORD BOOKWORMS LIBRARY offers a wide range of original and adapted stories, both classic and modern, which take learners from elementary to advanced level through six carefully graded language stages:

Stage 1 (400 headwords)	Stage 4 (1400 headwords)
Stage 2 (700 headwords)	Stage 5 (1800 headwords)
Stage 3 (1000 headwords)	Stage 6 (2500 headwords)

More than fifty titles are also available on cassette, and there are many titles at Stages 1 to 4 which are specially recommended for younger learners. In addition to the introductions and activities in each Bookworm, resource material includes photocopiable test worksheets and Teacher's Handbooks, which contain advice on running a class library and using cassettes, and the answers for the activities in the books.

Several other series are linked to the OXFORD BOOKWORMS LIBRARY. They range from highly illustrated readers for young learners, to playscripts, non-fiction readers, and unsimplified texts for advanced learners.

Oxford Bookworms Starters	*Oxford Bookworms Factfiles*
Oxford Bookworms Playscripts	*Oxford Bookworms Collection*

Details of these series and a full list of all titles in the OXFORD BOOKWORMS LIBRARY can be found in the *Oxford English* catalogues. A selection of titles from the OXFORD BOOKWORMS LIBRARY can be found on the next pages.

Death of an Englishman
MAGDALEN NABB
Retold by Diane Mowat

It was a very inconvenient time for murder. Florence was full of Christmas shoppers and half the police force was already on holiday.

At first it seemed quite an ordinary murder. Of course, there are always a few mysteries. In this case, the dead man had been in the habit of moving his furniture at three o'clock in the morning. Naturally, the police wanted to know why. The case became more complicated. But all the time, the answer was right under their noses. They just couldn't see it. It was, after all, a very ordinary murder.

The Big Sleep
RAYMOND CHANDLER
Retold by Rosalie Kerr

General Sternwood has four million dollars, and two young daughters, both pretty and both wild. He's an old, sick man, close to death, but he doesn't like being blackmailed. So he asks private detective Philip Marlowe to get the blackmailer off his back.

Marlowe knows the dark side of life in Los Angeles well, and nothing much surprises him. But the Sternwood girls are a lot wilder than their old father realizes. They like men, drink, drugs – and it's not just a question of blackmail.

BOOKWORMS • FANTASY & HORROR • STAGE 4
Dr Jekyll and Mr Hyde
ROBERT LOUIS STEVENSON
Retold by Rosemary Border

You are walking through the streets of London. It is getting dark and you want to get home quickly. You enter a narrow side-street. Everything is quiet, but as you pass the door of a large, windowless building, you hear a key turning in the lock. A man comes out and looks at you. You have never seen him before, but you realize immediately that he hates you. You are shocked to discover, also, that you hate him.

Who is this man that everybody hates? And why is he coming out of the laboratory of the very respectable Dr Jekyll?

BOOKWORMS • THRILLER & ADVENTURE • STAGE 4
The Thirty-Nine Steps
JOHN BUCHAN
Retold by Nick Bullard

'I turned on the light, but there was nobody there. Then I saw something in the corner that made my blood turn cold. Scudder was lying on his back. There was a long knife through his heart, pinning him to the floor.'

Soon Richard Hannay is running for his life across the hills of Scotland. The police are chasing him for a murder he did not do, and another, more dangerous enemy is chasing him as well – the mysterious 'Black Stone'. Who are these people? And why do they want Hannay dead?

The Moonspinners

MARY STEWART

Retold by Diane Mowat

When Nicola arrives in Crete a day early, she gets more than just an extra day of holiday. She comes to a village where no one can be trusted, and she becomes involved in a murder mystery that puts her own life in danger.

This story is set in a small village in the mountains of Crete. This is an island where people have strong feelings, where arguments begin suddenly, and end quickly. And Nicola has arrived in the middle of an argument that could end very quickly – with a gun.

The Dead of Jericho

COLIN DEXTER

Retold by Clare West

Chief Inspector Morse is drinking a pint of beer. He is thinking about an attractive woman who lives not far away.

The woman he is thinking of is hanging, dead, from the ceiling of her kitchen. On the floor lies a chair, almost two metres away from the woman's feet.

Chief Inspector Morse finishes his pint, and orders another. Perhaps he will visit Anne, after all. But he is in no particular hurry.

Meanwhile, Anne is still hanging in her kitchen, waiting for the police to come and cut her down. She is in no hurry, either.